A DIFFERENT KIND OF WEALTH

A Timely Guide Where History Is A Mirror, Inflection Points Are Lenses, Wealth Is Relational Power, And Community Is An Outcome.

A DIFFERENT KIND OF WEALTH

A Timely Guide Where History Is A Mirror, Inflection Points Are Lenses, Wealth Is Relational Power, And Community Is An Outcome.

DR. PAMELA C.V. JOLLY

wordeee
where words connect

A Different Kind of Wealth:
A Timely Guide Where History Is A Mirror, In!ection Points Are Lenses, Wealth Is Relational Power, And Community Is An Outcome.

ISBN: 978-1-967674-53-4 Hardcover
ISBN: 978-1-967674-32-9 eBook
Library of Congress Control Number: 2026908481

Print and eBook Layout Design: Amit Dey
Book Design: Pamela Jolly
Cover Design: Panagiotis Lampridis
Editor: A.J
Author's Photo Credit: Whitney Thomas

Website: www.wordeee.com
Twitter.com/wordeeeupdates
Facebook: facebook.com/Wordeee/
e-mail: contact@wordeee.com

Published by Wordeee in the United States, New York, New York
Printed in the USA

Other Books By Dr. Pamela Jolly.

The Narrow Road,
The Black Male Equity Initiative Anthpology:
Reclaiming the Dream,
The Sankofa View: Exploring Legacy as a Narrative,
The Wealth Finishing School.

- The NarrowRoad™ Guide to Legacy Wealth 1st Edition
- The NarrowRoad™ Guide to Legacy Wealth 2nd Edition
- The Sankofa View, Exploring Legacy as a Narrative
- The Black Male Equity Initiative Anthology, Detroit Reclaiming the Dream
- The NarrowRoad™ 2.0 The Journey To Wealth Your Way Journey 1: Casting Vision
- The NarrowRoad™ 2.0 The Journey To Wealth Your Way Journey 2: Defining Your Pursuit
- The NarrowRoad™ 2.0 The Journey To Wealth Your Way Journey 3: The Business of You
- The NarrowRoad™ 2.0 The Journey To Wealth Your Way Journey 4: The Business of Us
- The Wealth Finishing School, 12 Essential Steps to Building Wealth Your Way
- A Different Kind of Wealth

ADVANCE PRAISE

"Dr. Pamela Jolly offers a powerful reflection on how history, identity, and community intersect to shape generational opportunity. This book invites readers to understand their role in building a shared and prosperous future."

—Sheri Brady, Chief Operating Officer,
Children's Defense Fund

"*In A Different Kind of Wealth*, Dr. Pamela Jolly delivers a timely and insightful Sankofa-inspired guide for this generation, equipping readers with historical context to inform and shape a more purposeful vision for the future. The book thoughtfully challenges conventional narratives by inviting readers to reconsider their understanding of wealth, prosperity, and history, and to recognize how these elements collectively influence our path forward."

—Pastor Jonathan Chapman,
Church On Purpose, Omaha, NE

"Pamela Jolly has always embodied determination, clarity of thought, and an unwavering commitment to getting things done. From our earliest days growing up in Silver Spring, I have watched her approach challenges with both discipline and imagination. I am proud to call her my cousin, and even prouder of the work she continues to do."

—Malcolm Jolly,
Family Services Counselor

"*A Different Kind of Wealth offers* a powerful reminder that lasting prosperity is not built on financial capital alone, but on the wisdom we inherit from history and the perspective we bring to the future. By inviting readers to reflect on pivotal moments in American history and their own lived experience, the book challenges us to recognize how our unique differences can become an investment in the common good. It is a thoughtful and timely call to build wealth that endures, across generations, communities, and the future we share."

—Mandala Jones, Chief Executive Officer,
Housing Authority of Clayton County

"In a society where difference is either celebrated or crucified, Dr. Pamela Jolly instructs us how to channel difference through challenges into something that benefits communities. She uses both the rearview mirror and windshield simultaneously to show us everything we need to know to reach our financial visions."

—Dr. Tamecia Jones, College Professor

"*A Different Kind of Wealth* harnesses the power of perspective and teaches you how to convert that into an asset that builds monetary and emotional wealth for you and your community. Dr. Jolly's book is a must-read for anyone looking to break out of the trappings of mere survival and into a world of fulfillment."

—Hoyt King, Program Manager

"We live in a time when reflection and understanding of our place in the world have never been more critical. Our very fortunes seem to be balancing on the edge of a needle. This is a book that will do well in serving as a needed and powerful reminder. Let this writing encourage us to recall the Wisdom of our Forefathers and be Givers. May we all once again collectively pour into this glass that is our future, and just as before, be blessed."

—Whitney Thomas, Photographer

"For as long as I've known Pamela—and it has been nearly three decades now—she has devoted her heart, her mind, and her tireless energy to the pursuit of building wealth. Not for herself, but for the communities she so deeply loves and serves. Pamela brings to everything she touches a rare and remarkable combination of passion, discipline, and vision. It comes as no surprise, then, that she has channeled that same extraordinary spirit into the written word. I have no doubt that her latest literary work on wealth will be as rich in wisdom and purpose as the woman who wrote it—a true reflection of her lifelong commitment to uplifting others."

—Jacqueline Jenkins, Founder & Chief Curator,
Sophisticated Curatio

"Congratulations to my fellow Hamptonian, Dr. Pamela Jolly, for creating this powerful, bold, and insightful book that will surely help change the quality of life's trajectory of thousands of African Americans - forever. With clarity and inspiration, Dr. Jolly sheds light on key moments in America's history that shape our future and helps individuals understand their unique responsibility in defining, establishing, and sustaining legacy wealth. Imparting her wisdom to those of us who need it most, Dr. Jolly offers the gift of identifying and leveraging the opportunities that surround us."

—Calvin R. Ledford Jr., President, PSEG Foundation
& Director, Corporate Social Responsibility

"A *Different Kind of Wealth* provides a fresh viewpoint on history's impact and relationship to wealth for the reader, individually and in the context of one's greater community. Through a tangible and digestible 12-week exploration, Dr. Jolly empowers the audience to become an active participant and stakeholder in their uniquely individual journey to legacy wealth."

—Nia Jolly, Esq.
Assistnt District Attorney, Bronx County

Dr. Jolly delivers a compelling perspective on the evolving financial landscape, offering readers a rare combination of analytical depth, clarity, and actionable insight. This work stands out as an important voice in modern finance. She has written an exceptional resource that challenges conventional thinking while providing practical solutions for real-world financial leadership. Dr. Jolly provides readers with a clear, thoughtful, and forward-looking roadmap for navigating financial complexity with confidence and strategic vision. High Praise for her brilliant work A Different Kind of Wealth.

—Dr. Larry Frazier President/CEO
The FrazierGroup & Partners.

TABLE OF CONTENTS

FOREWORD

In 1776, Adam Smith published what became the foundational scripture of modern economic thought. The Wealth of Nations gave the world a framework, a way of naming what prosperity was, how it was created, and who, in theory, could pursue it. His invisible hand moved markets.

His division of labor multiplied production. His ideas toppled mercantilism and gave intellectual architecture to the capitalist age about to explode from the furnaces of the Industrial Revolution.

But Smith could not see what he could not see. His lens, brilliant as it was, had edges. It captured commerce but not the cost of those left out of it. It theorized freedom but lived inside a world where the labor of an entire people—stolen, uncompensated, compounded across generations—was the hidden engine beneath his elegant models. For all its genius, The Wealth of Nations was written by a man who could not yet name what it would cost us to ignore the wealth that difference makes. Two hundred and fifty years later, Dr. Pamela Jolly has written the book Smith could not.

She does not simply extend his argument. She corrects its omissions, expands its imagination, and invites every reader into a framework worthy of the moment we actually inhabit.

I say this not as flattery, though Dr. Jolly has earned every superlative that will be attached to this work. I say it because it is the most precise and honest thing I can offer at the beginning of a book that demands precision and honesty from its first page to its last. A Different Kind of Wealth is a seminal work. It will be studied. It will be assigned. It will be cited decades from now by economists, theologians, community architects, and the grandchildren of people who read it this year. The question is not whether this book matters. It is whether you are ready for what it asks of you.

THE SCOPE OF THE VISION

Dr. Jolly comes to this work the way great thinkers always do—not by accumulating credentials, but by accumulating truth. Four academic degrees. Decades of study across thousands of texts. A career spanning financial institutions, corporate boardrooms, faith communities, nonprofit systems, entrepreneurial ventures, and academic halls. She has not theorized wealth from a distance. She has sat in the rooms where wealth is protected, where it is denied, and where it is painstakingly built by people working with everything they have and half of what they deserve.

What she brings to this book is not an argument. It is a pattern—one she has seen repeat across generations, industries, cultures, and family trees. The pattern is this: people do not fail to build wealth because they lack ability. They fail because they have not yet fully owned their difference.

That insight, simple as it sounds, is revolutionary. It relocates the locus of transformation from external systems to internal clarity—not to deny that systems matter, but to insist that the person reading this page carries more power than they have been taught to believe. She equips us with a telescope and a microscope at once—to see across generations and to see deep into ourselves, simultaneously.

The twelve inflection points at the heart of this book are not history lessons. They are mirrors. Each one—from Jamestown in 1619 to the present—is a moment in which the American project revealed its fractures and its possibilities at the same time. Dr. Jolly moves through these moments not to wound us with the past but to equip us with its clarity. She understands what too few teachers do: that history is not a burden. History is a lens. And when you finally learn to see through it, you can see forward with a precision that no spreadsheet can match.

WHAT MAKES THIS DIFFERENT

There is no shortage of books about wealth. There are books about investing, about budgeting, about mindset, about hustle. Most of them, at their core, make the same implicit promise: follow this framework, and you will arrive at financial security. Some of them are useful. None of them are this.

A Different Kind of Wealth refuses the small promise. It is not a financial playbook —though its implications for how you handle money are profound. It is a philosophical, historical, and deeply personal reckoning with what wealth actually is, where it actually comes from, and what it is actually for. Dr. Jolly advances a definition that Smith never quite reached: wealth is relational power. It is not accumulated in isolation. It is not hoarded into permanence. It multiplies when it becomes collective. It endures when it carries the shape of the community that built it. You can get rich alone, she reminds us. But you cannot build anything that lasts alone. This is the crucial distinction. Accumulation fades. Legacy compounds. And legacy is built not from more money, but from more clarity about who you are, what you carry, and whom you are building toward.

We are the asset. What you carry—your gift, your genius, your particular way of seeing the world— is not a consolation prize. It is the investment waiting to be organized.

The structured twelve-week journey she offers is not a curriculum. It is a commissioning. She hands you a blueprint, places the tools in your hands, and draws a road map whose destination is not a number in an account but a generation shaped by your courage. The closing reflection—Do I believe I am worth investing in? —is not a soft question. It is the hardest question most of us will ever answer honestly.

The Arc That Becomes the Map. I have known Dr. Pamela Jolly long enough to understand that her work is not separable from her life. She has not written this book about a journey. She has written it from inside one—one that required her to inhabit the very questions she now poses to you. That is the rarest quality in any author, and it is what gives A Different Kind of Wealth its unmistakable texture. You can feel the lived weight behind every concept. You can sense the years of testimony, research, and honest reckoning that produced each insight.

She builds the arc with intention. It begins with Value, at 1619, the year that planted the epigenetic seed of both exploitation and resistance in the American story. It passes through Freedom, Perspective, Pivot, Pursuit, Partnership, Migration,

Patience, Alliance, Resurrection, Audacity, and arrives finally at Ownership—not merely financial ownership, but the psychological and generational freedom that comes when a person or a people takes full possession of their promised land. That arc is not accidental. It is a map. And maps, as every great explorer knows, do not tell you where to go. They show you where you are, what terrain lies ahead, and what it will require to cross it. America moves forward when people own their difference and organize it toward a shared outcome. It is not sameness that has carried us. It is aligned difference.

The glass partition of limitation, Dr. Jolly reminds us, has been moved. Each generation inherits a wider field of possibility than the one that preceded it—but only if those who came before were willing to push. This book is an act of pushing. It is an offering of the baton. It asks what you will do with the inheritance you have received, earned, and unearned, and what you will pass forward in its place.

A PERSONAL WORD

Friendship, at its best, gives you a front-row seat to someone's becoming. I have had that seat with Dr. Jolly, and what I can tell you is this: the person who wrote this book is the same person who lives it. She does not theorize conviction. She practices it. She does not preach collective investment. She embodies it, daily, in how she shows up for the people and communities she serves.

To be asked to write these words is an honor I do not take lightly. It is not simply an endorsement. It is a witness statement. I have watched this vision take shape across years of disciplined, courageous, faithful work. What you hold in your hands is not an accident. It is the fruit of a life fully committed to a question: What does it actually take for people to build wealth that lasts?

Her answer, finally in your hands, is not simple. But it is true. And in a moment saturated with noise and shortcuts and promises of ease, truth is the rarest and most valuable currency of all.

AN INVITATION

You are about to receive a telescope and a microscope at once. The telescope will show you the long arc of history bending toward the generation you are building. The microscope will show you, with uncomfortable clarity, the structures inside your own inheritance; what was given, what was withheld, and what remains yours to claim.

The transformation, Dr. Jolly is careful to tell us, happens in the space between — when you learn to see what is right in front of you. You are different, so that you can make a difference. Adam Smith told us that the wealth of nations is built through the invisible hand of free exchange. Dr. Pamela Jolly tells us what he could not: that the wealth of generations is built through the visible courage of people who own their difference, fund it with action, and offer it forward—not alone, but together. The future requires distributed courage. You are holding the blueprint.

Now build.

—Simon T. Bailey, Executive Advisor,
Researcher, and 12x Author

DEDICATION

This book is dedicated to the memory of my parents,
the late Vincent Creswell Jolly Sr.,
and the late Sylvia Mae Horne Jolly.

Their lives set the standard.

This work is my answer to that inheritance.

PROLOGUE

THE AMERICAN EXPERIMENT: WHY DIFFERENCE MATTERS NOW

America is different.

Not better.
Not worse.
Different.

From the beginning, this country has been an experiment; unfinished, audacious, and deeply contradictory. An experiment in whether people with different languages, faiths, cultures, classes, and histories could be bound together long enough to build something that outlived them.

For a time, the experiment worked.

It worked not because we agreed, but because enough people were willing to participate. Willing to take risks. Willing to invest labor, ideas, faith, capital, and conviction into something that did not yet exist.

America did not begin with certainty.
It began with belief:

Belief that freedom could be engineered.
Belief that markets could be built.
Belief that opportunity could expand.
Belief that the future could be shaped rather than inherited intact.

That belief—applied unevenly and often unjustly—produced extraordinary results. And now we stand at a familiar inflection point.

The experiment is strained.
Trust is thin.
Institutions feel brittle.
And many people are retreating into nostalgia, into fear, into isolation, and into sameness.

But history tells us something important:

> *America does not fail because it changes.*
> *America fails when people stop investing in the change.*

AN INHERITED ROLE

Every American—whether by birth, migration, or choice—has inherited a role in this experiment.

Not the same role.
Not an equal role.
But a role nonetheless.

Some inherited land.
Some inherited labor.
Some inherited advantage.
Some inherited trauma.
Some inherited faith strong enough to survive contradiction.

Some inherited systems designed to work for them. Others inherited the work of surviving systems that did not.

And yet, across four centuries, one pattern remains consistent:

America moves forward when people own their differences and organize them toward a shared outcome. It is not sameness that has carried us. It is an aligned difference.

Difference in perspective.
Difference in risk tolerance.
Difference in skill.
Difference in imagination.
Difference in what people are willing to sacrifice now for what they believe can exist later.

The experiment has always depended on people who were willing to bring *their* differences to the table, rather than waiting for permission to fit in.

WHAT HAS WON—AND WHAT WILL NOT

Let's be honest.

The systems that carried America to wealth and power worked, for a time. But many were built with incentives that concentrated ownership, monetized labor, protected property, and controlled access.

They rewarded participation, and they produced scale without requiring shared stewardship. That model is reaching its limit, not because wealth is scarce, but because ownership is uneven; not because capital is gone, but because trust is thin. And when trust thins, people don't stop building. They start building smaller, inside their own walls.

That model is exhausted.

Not because innovation has stopped, but because too many people feel disconnected from the outcome.

The next chapter of the American experiment will not be won by repeating the past louder.

It will be won by more people:

- Owning what they carry.
- Investing where they believe.
- And sharing their perspective with intention.

The future requires distributed courage.

A DIFFERENT KIND OF WEALTH

This is where a different kind of wealth comes in.

Not wealth defined only by money.
But wealth defined by:

- Capacity.
- Alignment.
- Collective intelligence.
- Intergenerational responsibility.

A wealth that understands:

- You can get rich alone.
- But you cannot build anything that lasts alone.

A wealth that recognizes:

- Your story matters.
- Your perspective is needed.
- And your difference is not a liability; it is an asset waiting to be organized.

The experiment does not need fewer differences.
It needs more people willing to name theirs.

THE INVITATION

This book is an invitation to step back into the experiment—not as a spectator, but as a steward.

To look at history honestly.
To look at yourself clearly.
And to decide how you will invest what you have inherited—both earned and unearned—into the future we are all shaping together.

Winning in the next chapter will require more of us:

- More ownership.
- More courage.
- More collaboration.
- More willingness to be seen.

The American experiment is still alive.

The question is not whether it will change.
It always does.

The question is whether you will participate, and whether you will bring your different kinds of wealth with you.

INTRODUCTION

My inflection point has a name. His name was Tommy.

When I was in third grade, Tommy called me the *n*-word. I didn't know what the word meant, but I knew—by the silence around us, by the way the air shifted—that something had just changed. I felt different before I understood why.

Like any child trying to make sense of the world, I went home and tested what I had learned. I called my father the same word, trying to understand its meaning through his reaction. What I didn't know then was that I had just stepped into a centuries-old inheritance—one carried in bodies, memories, and unspoken rules.

My father exploded. My mother did not.

My father believed he had earned the right for his daughter to grow up in a post-racial America. He wanted the world corrected.

My mother pulled me close and said, "Praise be to God, baby girl. You are Black. Now here are your African American flashcards."

That was the inflection point; everything changed. Not because I became different, but because I became aware of my difference.

From that day forward, Black history became one of the threads I used to stitch my life together. From all-white classrooms to Ivy League halls, from banking floors to seminary rooms, from entrepreneurship to research across more than one hundred cities, I learned this truth:

Being different is not bad. It is not better. But it is powerful.

Difference is not a flaw. It is a position.

And wealth—real wealth—is always shaped by perspective.

This book is not about becoming someone new. It is about taking full possession of who you already are.

It is about understanding how your inherited story—your culture, your faith, your fears, your ambitions—has shaped your view of money, risk, leadership, and freedom. And then learning how to convert that perspective into a different kind of wealth.

This is not a traditional history book, nor a conventional wealth guide. It is a journey through twelve inflection points, moments where belief, action, and collective consequence intersect. You are not asked to agree with every interpretation, but to locate yourself within the picture they form.

HOW TO USE THIS BOOK

This is a 12-week journey built around 12 historical inflection points.

Each chapter follows the same rhythm:

1. The Historical Mirror
2. The Internal Inflection
3. The Declaration (Coming Out as Different)
4. The Practice (Go Within)
5. The Share (Come Out)
6. The Action

Do not rush. Do not skip. Do not do this alone.

Wealth is a group process.

1619 – JAMESTOWN

What has always been there, waiting to be seen?

1776 – DECLARATION

What are you willing to risk to go your own way?

CONFLICT 1861 – 1865

What are you willing to risk to go your own way?

RECONSTRUCTION – 1865

Can you rebuild without becoming what broke you?

END OF ISOLATION – 1909

Who must partner with you for this to last?

YOU ARE DIFFERENT

A different kind of wealth goes beyond money; it's recognizing that your unique qualities, when invested, can fulfill the world's needs.

CHANGE YOU BELIEVE IN – 1896

What standard are you willing to live by?

ACCESS – 1954

Can you stay when the win is slow?

EXPANSION 1916 – 1930

What are you willing to leave to become who you are?

REPRESENTATION 1972 – 1980

What can rise after everthing falls?

PROTEST 1963 – 1968

Who must gather for the dream to scale?

TEST OF BELIEF 2008 – 2016

Do you believe the promise includes you?

LEGACY 2021 – 2024

What must be finished so others can build upon your legacy?

YOU ARE DIFFERENT

A different kind of wealth goes beyond money; it's recognizing that your unique qualities, when invested, can fulfill the world's needs.

1619 — JAMESTOWN

What has always been there, waiting to be seen?

CHAPTER 1

SEEING YOUR VALUE—UNDERSTANDING WHY NOW

INFLECTION POINT 1: 1619

THE MOMENT BEFORE THE STORY BEGINS

Every journey has a beginning that feels invisible at the time.

You don't notice it when you're standing in it.
You only recognize it later—when everything that followed suddenly makes sense.

For America, that inflection point is 1619.

Not because it was the first ship.
Not because it was the first colony.
But because it marked the moment value was assigned, extracted, and normalized in ways that would echo for centuries.

Before America was a nation, it was an idea struggling to survive. And before it was an idea, it was a business problem.

Jamestown was failing.

Of the roughly 9,000 people who sailed to Virginia in the early years, only about 1,000 survived. Disease, starvation, poor planning, and outdated assumptions were killing the dream faster than it could take root. The settlers had brought old tools, old habits, and old leadership models into a new world that required something different.

The problem wasn't effort.
The problem was perspective.

The settlers were doing what humanity had done for more than 5,000 years—farming with the same tools, organizing labor communally, assuming survival would come from sameness rather than strategy. They believed everyone would give what they could and take what they needed, and that goodwill would be enough.

It wasn't.

Jamestown did not begin to stabilize until leadership made a controversial shift: connecting value to responsibility and production to ownership. When people were allowed to benefit directly from their labor, behavior changed. Productivity increased. Survival followed.

This pivot saved the colony.

And it installed the first operating logic of American wealth:

> *Value must be recognized before it can be protected.*

That lesson has never stopped repeating.

1619 AND THE PRICE OF UNSEEN VALUE

In the same year Jamestown began to find its footing, another ship arrived.

This one carried human beings who were not seen as settlers, partners, or stakeholders, but as assets.

What arrived in 1619 was not just people.
It was a valuation decision.

African bodies were assigned economic value without moral recognition. Skills, strength, agricultural knowledge, craftsmanship, and endurance were extracted while humanity was denied. This created what would become America's first—and longest-lasting—unfair competitive advantage.

For 276 years, enslaved Africans and their descendants would be the largest asset on America's balance sheet.

This is not metaphor.
It is accounting.

And here is where Inflection Point 1 becomes personal.

Because the most dangerous form of undervaluation is not when others fail to see your worth.

It is when you internalize it.

The 1619 inflection is not only about slavery or colonization. It is about what happens when value is defined externally for so long that entire generations struggle to name it internally.

This pattern helps explain some modern dynamics around money, confidence, leadership, risk, and belief—especially in communities shaped by long exposure to external valuation.

When value is assigned without consent, survival becomes the goal.
When survival becomes the goal, vision shrinks.
When vision shrinks, wealth becomes transactional instead of generational.

1619 asks a question that every reader must answer before moving forward:

> *Do you see your value—or are you negotiating against it?*

THE UNSEEN RULES OF CULTURE

Every culture has rules within rules.

Unwritten expectations.
Invisible boundaries.
Unspoken pathways that reward some behaviors and punish others.

If you were raised inside those rules, they feel normal. If you weren't raised inside those rules, they can feel arbitrary or costly. This is why two people can walk the same road and experience entirely different outcomes.

The unseen rules shape how value is:

- Recognized.
- Rewarded.
- Protected.
- Passed on.

When you don't know the rules, you may appear the same while being treated differently. And when you finally realize the difference, it can feel destabilizing—like discovering mid-journey that the map you were given was incomplete.

This is not a personal failure.
It is a historical inheritance.

1619 marks the moment when American culture began assigning radically different meanings to the same concepts: work, freedom, ownership, and worth.

Those meanings did not disappear with emancipation. They evolved. Which is why Inflection Point 1 is not about blame.

It is about clarity.

You cannot build wealth—of any kind—without first understanding the value system you are operating within.

And you cannot change that system until you see your place in it.

SEEING YOURSELF AS THE ASSET

Along the NarrowRoad™, seeing is believing, and belief always must come before anything meaningful happens.

Not optimism.
Not motivation.
Belief.

Belief is what determines action.
Action is what requires ownership.

And ownership begins with position.

Here is the truth most people never say out loud:

You are the asset before you ever make an asset.

Your ability.
Your genius.
Your skill.
Your talent.
Your promise.

These are not abstract qualities. They are economic drivers when you believe in them enough to act. But belief is fragile when history has taught you to doubt yourself.

That doubt may show up as:

- Overworking.
- Undercharging.
- Avoiding risk.
- Playing small.
- Seeking permission.
- Confusing security with safety.

These patterns are not personal flaws.
They are inherited adaptations.

1619 is where those adaptations begin.

And it is also where they can end.

THE PERSONAL INFLECTION: BECOMING AWARE

For me, this awareness came early.

His name was Tommy.

In third grade, Tommy called me the *n*-word. I didn't understand the word, but I understood the moment. The silence. The heat. The shift.

When I went home and tested the word on my father, I watched centuries of inheritance surface in seconds. My father's rage. My mother's tenderness. Two different strategies for survival. Two different relationships with belief.

That day, I learned something most people learn much later:

Difference is not discovered—it is revealed.

And once revealed, it demands a response.

You can deny it.
You can hide it.
You can try to outrun it.
Or you can own it.

That choice—to own your difference—is the first real act of wealth-building. Because once you see your value, you cannot unsee it.

THE DECLARATION OF VALUE

Every inflection point requires a declaration.

Not a public performance.
An internal line in the sand.

This is where belief becomes action.

Declaration—Inflection Point 1

> *I see my value.*
> *I believe in it.*
> *I will no longer negotiate against myself.*

This declaration does not change the world immediately. It changes you.

And that is where all durable change begins.

PRACTICE: THE FIRST ACT OF OWNERSHIP

This week's work is intentionally simple and intentionally uncomfortable.

Because value is not proven in grand gestures.
It is revealed in alignment.

Practice—Go Within.

Choose one area of your life where you have been:

- Underestimating yourself.
- Overcompensating.
- Accepting less than you know you deserve.

Do one thing that aligns with your value.

Not performative.
Not dramatic.
Aligned.

That might mean:

- Saying no.
- Asking for clarity.
- Charging appropriately.
- Taking rest seriously.
- Naming your contribution.

Write it down.
Notice how it feels.

Discomfort is often a sign you're changing a long-held pattern. Notice it. Write down what it's trying to teach you.

SHARING THE DIFFERENCE

Wealth is never built in isolation.

Your next step is to share—not convince.

Choose one person you trust and tell them what you saw about your value this week. Not your résumé. Not your results.

Your realization.

This is your first act of "coming out as different."

And it matters more than you think.

Because once value is named aloud, it begins to organize itself.

WHY THIS MATTERS NOW

1619 is not the past.

It is the foundation beneath every modern conversation about work, worth, equity, leadership, and opportunity.

We are living at an inflection point where old systems are cracking—not because people are weak, but because belief has shifted.

People are no longer willing to participate in systems that require them to disappear.

This is not rebellion.
It is recalibration.

And it begins the same way it always has:

With someone deciding to see their value—and act accordingly.

CLOSING REFLECTION

Before you can declare independence...
Before you can pursue perspective...
Before you can build strategy...
Before you can find your people...

You must answer one question honestly:

> *Do I believe I am worth investing in?*

1619 invites you to say yes.

And to mean it.

BEFORE MOVING FORWARD, NOTICE WHERE THIS INFLECTION ALREADY LIVES IN YOUR LIFE. WHAT FEELS INHERITED? WHAT FEELS CHOSEN?

1776 — DECLARATION

What are you willing to risk to go your own way?

CHAPTER 2

DECLARING YOUR INDEPENDENCE OWNING YOUR POSITION

INFLECTION POINT 2: 1776

FREEDOM BEGINS BEFORE IT IS ANNOUNCED

Independence is often remembered as a moment.

A declaration.
A document.
A date on a calendar.

But in reality, independence begins long before it is announced.

It begins internally—quietly—when a person or a people decide that continuing as they are costs more than the risk of change.

By the time America declared independence in 1776, the decision had already been made.

The Declaration of Independence did not *create* freedom. It named a belief that had been forming for years.

And belief—along the NarrowRoad™—always comes before action.

THE REAL WORK OF 1776

The popular story of 1776 focuses on courage, liberty, and vision. And those things matter.

But underneath the language of ideals was a harder truth:

The colonies were no longer willing to outsource their future.

They were tired of taxation without representation.
Tired of rules made by people who would never live with the consequences.
Tired of being productive without being powerful.

Sound familiar?

The American Revolution was not just political.
It was economic.
It was strategic.
It was psychological.

It was a refusal to continue participating in a system that benefited from their labor while denying their voice.

This is the second lesson of wealth:

> *Independence requires ownership of belief.*

Not consensus.
Not approval.
Ownership.

THE COST OF DECLARING INDEPENDENCE

Here is the part of the story we often sanitize:

Declaring independence was dangerous.

The men who signed the Declaration were not guaranteed victory. They were guaranteed risk. Loss. Retaliation. Ruin.

They were signing their names to a future that did not yet exist.

This matters because independence is often romanticized, but rarely contextualized.

Independence is not freedom from responsibility.
It is the **acceptance of greater responsibility**.

When you declare independence, you also accept a new relationship to outcomes: more choice, more accountability, more consequence.

Freedom doesn't eliminate constraints, but it does clarify what you can influence, what you must decide, and what you can no longer postpone.

This is why many people say they want freedom, but hesitate when it is time to choose it.

Because freedom removes excuses.

INTERNAL EMANCIPATION

Along the NarrowRoad™, independence is not a rebellion against others.

It is an emancipation from outsourcing your beliefs.

Many people face real constraints.

Many people are also un-positioned.

Freedom expands fastest when we name both: what is real, and what is changeable.

Most people are not unfree because they are oppressed. They are unfree because they are un-positioned.

They have not decided:

- What they believe.
- What they are willing to risk.
- What they will no longer tolerate.
- What they are responsible for building.

Without those decisions, movement feels dangerous, even when the current situation is unsustainable.

1776 teaches us this:

You cannot inherit independence.
You must declare it.
And every declaration has consequences.

THE INCOMPLETE PROMISE

Here is the tension we must name honestly.

America declared independence while maintaining slavery. It proclaimed liberty while denying it to women, Indigenous peoples, and the enslaved.

This contradiction does not invalidate the declaration.
It exposes its incompleteness.

The founders declared independence for themselves—not for everyone.

And that unfinished work is not a failure of the experiment.

It is its inheritance.

Every generation is handed a partially fulfilled promise and asked the same question:

> *Will you expand it—or protect it as is?*

1776 was a beginning, not a conclusion.

THE PERSONAL PARALLEL

Independence moments show up in individual lives the same way they show up in history.

You reach a point where:

- The rules no longer fit.
- The expectations feel misaligned.
- The cost of staying feels heavier than the risk of leaving.

It might be a job.
A belief system.
A relationship.
A financial pattern.
A family role.
An identity that once protected you but now confines you.
And yet, even when clarity comes, many people hesitate.

Because declaring independence means saying:
"This is my responsibility now."

That sentence terrifies people more than uncertainty ever could.

INDEPENDENCE IS NOT ISOLATION

One of the greatest misunderstandings about independence is the belief that it means doing everything alone.

It does not.

The American colonies did not fight alone.
They formed alliances.
They leveraged partnerships.
They pooled resources.

Independence is not withdrawal.

It is self-definition within a relationship.

Along the NarrowRoad™, independence means you stop borrowing your beliefs—but you do not stop collaborating.

You choose your position so that partnership becomes intentional, not accidental.

THE DECLARATION OF INDEPENDENCE (PERSONAL EDITION)

At this inflection point, you are not asked to burn bridges.

You are asked to name your stance.

To stop living by default.
To stop drifting.
To stop pretending neutrality is safety.

Declaration – Inflection Point 2

> *I declare my independence.*
> *I own my difference.*
> *I accept responsibility for my beliefs, my actions, and my outcomes.*

This declaration is not loud.
It is firm.

PRACTICE: THE FIRST INDEPENDENT ACT

Independence is proven through action—not intention.

Practice—Go Within.

Identify one area of your life where you have been:

- Waiting for permission.
- Deferring to others' expectations.
- Avoiding a clear decision.

Take one independent action this week.

Not reckless.
Not reactive.

Independent.

That might look like:

Making a decision without polling everyone

Setting a boundary

Choosing a direction instead of keeping options open

Ending something that has already expired.

Write down what you did—and what fear tried to stop you.

Fear is not a warning sign.
It is often confirmation that independence is near.

SHARING THE DECLARATION

Independence becomes real when it is spoken.

Choose one trusted person and share:

- What you are declaring independence from.
- What you are choosing to own.

Do not justify.
Do not over-explain.

Just state it.

You are not asking for approval.
You are practicing alignment.

WHY 1776 STILL MATTERS

We live in a moment where many people feel disillusioned with institutions, systems, and leaders.

That disillusionment is not new.

What is new is the scale.

1776 reminds us that progress does not begin with perfect systems.

It begins with people who are willing to take responsibility for what they believe and act accordingly.

Independence is not a historical event.

It is a recurring decision.

CLOSING REFLECTION

Before you can pursue your perspective...
Before you can navigate conflict...
Before you can build strategy...
Before you can find your collective...

You must answer this question honestly:

> *What am I willing to own—without guarantee of success?*

1776 invites you to answer with action.

BEFORE MOVING FORWARD, NOTICE WHERE THIS INFLECTION ALREADY LIVES IN YOUR LIFE. WHAT FEELS INHERITED? WHAT FEELS CHOSEN?

CONFLICT 1861 – 1865

What are you willing to risk to go your own way?

CHAPTER 3

PURSUING YOUR PERSPECTIVE: CONFLICT, UNION, AND THE COURAGE TO BE SET APART

INFLECTION POINT 3: 1861

WHEN CONFLICT BECOMES INEVITABLE

There are inflection points in history—and in life—when conflict is no longer avoidable.

Not because people suddenly become unreasonable.
But because two incompatible visions are trying to occupy the same future.

By 1861, America had reached that point.

The nation was no longer arguing about policy.
It was arguing about **purpose**.

What kind of country was this going to be?
Who would benefit from its growth?
Whose labor counted—and whose life?

The Civil War did not begin because people failed to compromise.

It began because compromise had been stretched beyond its moral and economic limits.

This is the inflection point where America learned a painful but necessary lesson:

Union without shared perspective eventually collapses.
And so does any life built the same way.

THE ILLUSION OF AVOIDABLE CONFLICT

We like to believe that conflict is a failure of communication.

If we could just talk better.
Listen harder.
Be more patient.

But some conflicts are not misunderstandings.
They are **misalignments**.

By 1861, the North and the South were not disagreeing on tactics. They were operating from entirely different economic and moral frameworks.

The South's prosperity depended on enslaved labor.
The North's growth depended on expansion, industry, and global legitimacy.

One side was invested in preservation.
The other in progress.

Both claimed loyalty to the Union.

But only one was willing to change.

This is why conflict erupted, not as a breakdown, but as a reckoning.

PERSPECTIVE IS NOT NEUTRAL

Here is where Inflection Point 3 becomes deeply personal.

Most people believe they are neutral.
They believe they are "just trying to keep the peace."

But neutrality is not the absence of perspective.
It is the protection of the status quo.

In moments of moral or strategic tension, choosing not to choose is still a choice.

The Civil War forces us to confront an uncomfortable truth:

> *Perspective has consequences.*

What you see determines what you protect.
What you protect determines what survives.

This applies to nations—and to individuals.

BEING SET APART

Freedom has always had a separating effect.

When enslaved people pursued freedom, they were separated from what they knew.

When abolitionists pursued justice, they were separated from comfort.

When the nation pursued unity, it was separated from illusion.

The journey from bondage to freedom always creates distance.

This is why Inflection Point 3 is not about fighting to win.

It is about **owning your difference within conflict**.

Being a "square peg in a round hole" is not a design flaw.
It is often a signal that you are carrying a perspective the system has not yet learned how to hold.

TRAUMA, DUALITY, AND THE LONG MEMORY

In seminary, I learned something that reshaped how I see history and people.

Trauma does not stay where it begins.
It moves—sometimes like a spirit—from one generation to the next.

A generation does not have to experience an event to inherit its impact.

America's Civil War left more than battlefields and graves.
It left unresolved trauma embedded in systems, institutions, and relationships.

This trauma explains why:

- Conflict resurfaces around the same issues.
- Fear is triggered faster than reason.
- Progress feels cyclical instead of linear.

But trauma also carries information.

If we are willing to look back honestly, we can learn how to move forward differently.

This is what I call the **Sankofa View**: the understanding that the way forward is back *through*.

THE GAP THAT DEFINES THE JOURNEY

At the heart of the Civil War was a gap.

A gap between:

- Promise and practice.
- Freedom declared, and freedom lived.
- Union claimed and union embodied.

Every generation inherits that gap.

Some try to ignore it.
Some try to close it by force.
Others learn how to **build across it**.

This is where a different kind of wealth is formed.

Because wealth is not just what you accumulate.
It is what you learn to carry responsibly across generations.

AMERICA AS A BUSINESS—AND YOU AS ONE TOO

Here is a framing that often changes how people see themselves:

Your life is a business.

You are the primary asset.
Your habits are the operating system.
Your choices determine return.

America is also a business.

Its citizens are its shareholders.
Its systems are its infrastructure.

Its success depends on whether enough people are aligned around a shared purpose.

The Civil War was a hostile takeover attempt of the nation's future.

The question was not whether America would survive.

It was what kind of America would survive.

The same question shows up in our lives at moments of deep conflict.

RISK IS NOT EXPERIENCED EQUALLY

Conflict exposes inequality.

Risk emboldens some people and paralyzes others.
Change motivates some and terrifies others.

This is why perspective matters.

People experience the same moment differently depending on:

- What they have to lose.
- What they have already endured.
- What they believe is possible.

A different kind of wealth recognizes this—and does not try to flatten experience into one story.

THE DECLARATION OF PERSPECTIVE

Inflection Point 3 asks for something more difficult than independence.

It asks for courage in conflict.

Not to dominate.
Not to disappear.
But to stand.

Declaration — Inflection Point 3

> *I will pursue my perspective.*
> *Even when it creates tension.*
> *Even when it costs me comfort.*
> *Even when reconciliation takes time.*

This is not a declaration of war.
It is a declaration of integrity.

PRACTICE: NAMING THE CONFLICT

Avoidance delays freedom.

Practice — Go Within.

Name the conflict you have been avoiding.

Not the surface issue—the real one.

Ask yourself:

- What truth am I holding back?
- Where am I staying silent to stay safe?
- What perspective am I afraid to own?

Write it down.

Clarity is not cruel.
It is corrective.

SHARING ACROSS THE DIVIDE

Reconciliation is not agreement.

It is **movement**.

Choose one person connected to this conflict and share your perspective—not to convince, but to be seen.

Say:
"This is how I see it."
"This is what I'm choosing to own."

Let the outcome unfold.

Union cannot be forced.
But it can be invited.

WHY 1861 STILL LIVES WITH US

Every generation faces its own version of 1861.

Moments when systems no longer hold.
When silence becomes complicity.
When unity demands truth.

We are living in such a moment now.

The lesson of 1861 is not that conflict is bad.

It is that **unexamined conflict is destructive**.

But conflict owned with perspective can move us forward.

CLOSING REFLECTION

Before you can pivot strategically...
Before you can build alliances...
Before you can find your people...

You must answer this question:

> *What perspective am I willing to stand in—without knowing how it will be received?*

1861 invites you to stand anyway.

BEFORE MOVING FORWARD, NOTICE WHERE THIS INFLECTION ALREADY LIVES IN YOUR LIFE. WHAT FEELS INHERITED? WHAT FEELS CHOSEN?

RECONSTRUCTION — 1865

Can you rebuild without becoming what broke you?

CHAPTER 4

STRATEGY, RECONSTRUCTION, AND THE POWER OF THE PIVOT

INFLECTION POINT 4: 1865

FREEDOM WITHOUT STRATEGY IS FRAGILE

1865 did not bring peace.

It brought **possibility**, and with it, danger.

The Civil War ended, but the work did not. In many ways, it had just begun. The nation had won the war, but it had not yet secured the future. Freedom had been declared, but it had not been operationalized.

This is the first hard lesson of Reconstruction:

> *Victory without strategy creates vulnerability.*

The same is true in our lives.

Many people experience a breakthrough—a promotion, a divorce, a degree, a diagnosis, a calling, a revelation—and mistake the end of one struggle for the beginning of ease.

But freedom is not self-sustaining.

It must be **structured**.

RECONSTRUCTION WAS NEVER ABOUT CONSTRUCTION

Reconstruction is often misunderstood.

It was not about building something new from scratch.
It was about **rebuilding under pressure**, while grief was still raw, while resentment was still active, while systems were still contested.

Construction is hard.
Reconstruction is harder.

Construction assumes alignment.
Reconstruction assumes resistance.

Reconstruction requires:

- Negotiation instead of imagination.
- Strategy instead of sentiment.
- Endurance instead of enthusiasm.

This is why Inflection Point 4 is about **headwinds**.

HEADWINDS ARE NOT PUNISHMENT

A headwind is not a failure.

It is resistance encountered while moving forward.

When the wind is at your back, momentum feels natural. You begin to believe the pace will last. You plan as if progress is permanent.

But when the wind shifts—and it always does—everything changes.

Seth Godin writes that headwinds feel endless only when we forget they shift.

History confirms this.

Every major expansion of freedom in America has been followed by resistance:

- The end of slavery.
- The Reconstruction Amendments.
- Desegregation.
- Civil Rights legislation.
- Voting access.
- Political representation.

Progress creates pushback.

Not because it is wrong—but because it redistributes power.

1865: THE PIVOT POINT

In 1865, America faced a strategic choice.

Would it:

- Invest in rebuilding relationships as well as infrastructure?
- Create systems to support newly freed people as economic participants?
- Redesign its business model for freedom, not just labor?

Or would it:

- Rush reconciliation.
- Skip capacity-building.
- Assume freedom would "work itself out"?

We know what happened.

The nation chose speed over structure.

And in doing so, it left gaps that still haunt us.

THE COST OF SKIPPED STEPS

Reconstruction produced remarkable achievements:

- The 13th, 14th, and 15th Amendments.
- The Freedmen's Bureau.
- Civil Rights legislation.

But it also skipped two critical steps.

First, there was no **business model for freedom**.

Formerly enslaved people were emancipated without capital, protection, or access to ownership. Freedom was granted, but infrastructure was withheld.

Second, there was no **strategy for inclusion**.

Federal protection was temporary. Integration was assumed. Resistance was underestimated.

These omissions did not just slow progress.

They shaped generations.

WHAT THIS TEACHES US PERSONALLY

Most people fail not because they lack vision, but because they underestimate the importance of **strategy after the breakthrough.**

They escape something harmful...
But don't build toward something sustainable.

They pivot emotionally...
But not structurally.

They change direction...
But not habits.

This is why Reconstruction matters to you.

Because every life has a Reconstruction season.

A moment when:

- You've left what no longer works.
- You've survived something difficult.
- You've earned a new kind of freedom.

And now the question is:

> *What strategy will carry you forward?*

NEGOTIATION OVER DESERVING

Reconstruction teaches another uncomfortable truth:

> *What you deserve is not always what determines outcomes.*
> *What you negotiate determines outcomes.*

The formerly enslaved deserved land, safety, and opportunity.

But without leverage, without structure, without sustained protection, "deserving" was not enough.

This is not cynicism.
It is reality.
And it applies to all of us.

THE PIVOT IS NOT THE END—IT'S THE BEGINNING

A pivot is not panic.

It is recalibration.

Reconstruction required America to pivot from extraction to development, from domination to governance, from tradition to transformation.

It failed in many ways—not because the pivot was unnecessary, but because it was incomplete.

This is where Inflection Point 4 becomes instructional.

A pivot without follow-through is just movement.

Strategy turns movement into momentum.

THE PERSONAL HEADWINDS YOU MUST READ

Headwinds show up personally as:

- Resistance after clarity.
- Fatigue after commitment.
- Pushback after progress.
- Doubt after decision.

These are not signs to stop.
They are signals to **adjust**.

Ask yourself:

- What systems need strengthening?
- What relationships require renegotiation?
- What habits must change to support my freedom?

Freedom without structure collapses under pressure.

DECLARATION – INFLECTION POINT 4

> *I will be strategic.*
> *I will not confuse freedom with ease.*
> *I will pivot with intention and build for endurance.*

This is not about perfection.

It is about **positioning**.

PRACTICE: THE STRATEGIC INVENTORY

Go Within.

Identify:

1. One **area** where you have experienced freedom—but lack structure.
2. One **headwind** you've been resisting instead of reading.
3. One **pivot** you've avoided because it requires learning something new.

Write it down.

Strategy begins with honesty.

SHARING: NEGOTIATING FORWARD

Choose one trusted person and say:

"I'm rebuilding this part of my life. I'm learning to be strategic about it."

This is not a confession.

It is a commitment.

WHY 1865 STILL MATTERS

We live in a time that celebrates disruption but resists reconstruction.

We praise visionaries and neglect builders.
We honor breakthroughs and ignore systems.

But history teaches us this:

> *Freedom that lasts is designed—not assumed.*

Reconstruction was not a failure because freedom was wrong.

It struggled because strategy was **unfinished**.

Your life does not have to repeat that pattern.

CLOSING REFLECTION

Before you can pursue change you believe in...
Before you can form alliances...
Before you can build collectively...

You must answer this:

> *What strategy will support the freedom I've claimed?*

1865 invites you to build—not just break free.

BEFORE MOVING FORWARD, NOTICE WHERE THIS INFLECTION ALREADY LIVES IN YOUR LIFE. WHAT FEELS INHERITED? WHAT FEELS CHOSEN?

CHANGE YOU BELIEVE IN – 1896

What standard are you willing to live by?

CHAPTER 5

PURSUING CHANGE YOU BELIEVE IN—ALLIANCE, RISK, AND THE COURAGE TO BUILD

INFLECTION POINT 5: 1896

WHEN PROGRESS REVERSES—AND CLARITY BECOMES COSTLY

1896 was not a beginning.

It was a return.

A return to what was familiar.
A return to what felt controllable.
A return to what those in power could justify.

Plessy v. Ferguson did not invent separation.
It **codified retreat**.

After three decades of halting progress, incomplete **reconstruction**, and fragile gains, the Supreme Court declared what many already wanted to believe: *separate but equal.*

It was a ruling about trains.
But it was really a ruling about **belonging**.

And this is why Inflection Point 5 matters so deeply, then and now.

Because it marks the moment when people had to decide.

> *Do I wait for systems to catch up... or do I build what I believe in anyway?*

BONDAGE IS NOT ONLY EXTERNAL

By 1896, slavery was over.
But bondage was not.

Bondage simply changed form.

It moved inward—into:

- Expectations.
- Permissions.
- Internalized limits.
- Negotiated silence.

This is one of the hardest truths in the pursuit of freedom.

> *You can exit a position and still carry its logic.*

Bondage becomes the story you tell yourself about what's possible.
About how much you can ask for.
About who will support you.
About whether it's worth the risk.

Inflection Point 5 asks you to confront that story.

DEGREES OF FREEDOM

After emancipation, freedom did not arrive as a single experience.

It came in **degrees.**

Some migrated.
Some sharecropped.
Some pooled resources.
Some built institutions.

Everyone was on the same road, but not in the same lane.
And this is critical:

> *Your degree of desired freedom determines how you define expansion.*

Some people want safety.
Others want ownership.
Others want influence.
Others want legacy.

None is wrong.

But confusion arises when you pursue one degree of freedom using the tools of another.

THE CHAOS OF BUILDING SOMETHING NEW

1896 initiated a building period—not sanctioned by the state, but fueled by necessity.

When systems close doors, people build side entrances.

This era produced:

- Black colleges and universities.
- Mutual aid societies.
- Fraternal organizations.
- Faith-based economic networks.
- Social capital as protection.

This was not accidental.

It was strategic.

And it reveals a timeless principle:

> *When clarity becomes dangerous, community becomes currency, and wealth becomes a collective pursuit of permanence.*

INTERNAL AND EXTERNAL ALLIANCE

Inflection Point 5 introduces a shift from independence to **alliance**.

Not assimilation.
Not dependence.
But alignment.

This is where the *Business of You* meets the *Business of Us*.

An alliance requires:

- Clarity about your needs.
- Honesty about your limits.
- Courage to be seen.
- Willingness to risk disappointment.

And most importantly:

Belief must drive action, and action requires ownership of your position.

You cannot outsource conviction.

THE FOUR RISKS THAT SHAPE THIS SEASON

This is where many people get stuck, not because they lack vision, but because they misread risk.

Four risks are operating at this inflection point.

Residual Risk
Lingering patterns that once protected you but now restrict growth.

Systemic Risk
Structures that advantage some and constrain others, regardless of effort.

Positional (Strategic) Risk
The vulnerability that comes with repositioning yourself before you feel "ready."

Legacy Risk
The fear of breaking the story you inherited—or being responsible for rewriting it.

Each risk asks a question.

The wrong response is avoidance.
The right response is alignment.

FAITH AS THE FIFTH RISK

There is a fifth risk rarely named.

Faith.

Faith is not blind optimism.
It is disciplined trust.

Faith risk appears when:

- The numbers don't add up yet.
- The support hasn't materialized.
- The vision is clear, but the path is not.

Faith risk teaches you something systems cannot:

Who you are when certainty is unavailable.

This is why post-Reconstruction wealth became collective.

Faith had to be shared to survive.

> *Faith risk when taken becomes an unblinded faithwalk.*

PURSUING EQUALITY DIFFERENTLY

1896 forced a reframing.

If equality would not be delivered uniformly, then it would have to be pursued strategically.

This is where equity begins, not as entitlement, but as intentional design.

Funding the win requires:

- Identifying the winner inside you.
- Choosing the strategy that fits *your* position.
- Releasing the need to be understood by everyone.

Progress is not permission-based.

THE MYTH OF SELF-HATRED AND THE WORK OF KNOWING YOURSELF

There is a quote that says, "Any attempt to change yourself is rooted in self-hatred."

That sounds poetic.
It is also incomplete.

The truth is this:

> *Most people are not trying to change*
> *because they hate themselves.*
> *They are trying to change because they don't fully*
> *know themselves.*

Not knowing yourself creates overcompensation.
Overcompensation creates exhaustion.
Exhaustion creates distance from people you love and from yourself.

This is internal bondage.

Inflection Point 5 asks you to stop performing and start aligning.

CREATING A NEW LETTER FOR THE ALPHABET

Change you believe in often looks impossible at first.

Like creating a new letter for the alphabet.

It exists clearly in your mind, but not yet in the world.

Others may not see it.
Some may dismiss it.
Some may fear it.

That does not make it wrong.

It makes it **yours**.

And ownership is the price of innovation.

DECLARATION – INFLECTION POINT 5

> *I will pursue change I believe in.*
> *I will build standards that include my needs.*
> *I will align with people who strengthen my vision.*
> *I will stop waiting for permission.*

This declaration is not loud.
It is durable.

PRACTICE: IDENTIFYING THE ALLIANCE

Go Within.

Answer honestly:

- What change do I believe in but have not yet pursued?
- What risk am I avoiding because it might expose me?

- What alliance would make this possible—but requires vulnerability?

Write it down.

Clarity precedes courage.

SHARING: NAMING YOUR STANDARD

Choose one person and say:

"This is the standard I'm building toward. I don't need **agreement**, I need alignment."

Then listen.

Alliances reveal themselves quickly.

WHY 1896 IS STILL WITH US

Whenever progress threatens comfort, regression disguises itself as tradition.

1896 reminds us:

> *History does not move forward automatically.*
> *It moves forward because people decide to build anyway.*

You are one of those people, or you are waiting for them.

CLOSING REFLECTION

Before you can find your wealth collective...
Before you can build across differences...
Before you can expand beyond survival...

You must answer this:

> *What change am I willing to pursue—even if it makes me stand apart?*

1896 invites you to build with belief.

BEFORE MOVING FORWARD, NOTICE WHERE THIS INFLECTION ALREADY LIVES IN YOUR LIFE. WHAT FEELS INHERITED? WHAT FEELS CHOSEN?

END OF ISOLATION – 1909

Who must partner with you for this to last?

CHAPTER 6

FINDING YOUR WEALTH COLLECTIVE: PARTNERSHIP, PURSUIT, AND THE END OF ISOLATION

INFLECTION POINT 6: 1909

WEALTH IS NEVER A SOLO ACT

By 1909, something critical had become undeniable.

No matter how gifted, determined, or disciplined a person might be, **no one builds enduring wealth alone**.

Individuals can accumulate money in isolation.
But wealth—real wealth—requires **relationship**.

This is the lesson of 1909.

It is the moment when survival strategies mature into **collective pursuit**.

And it is where many modern wealth builders quietly stall because they try to win alone what history has always required a group to sustain.

THE MYTH OF SELF-MADE SUCCESS

America loves the myth of the self-made individual.

It is clean.
It is simple.
And it is incomplete.

Every so-called self-made success story rests on invisible scaffolding:

- Teachers.
- Institutions.
- Networks.
- Timing.
- Inherited access or inherited resistance.

The question is not whether help exists. The question is whether you can see it, accept it, and steward it.

1909 marks the recognition that progress without partnership is fragile.

A SHIFT FROM INDEPENDENCE TO INTERDEPENDENCE

Up to this point in the journey:

- 1619 taught us value.
- 1776 taught us independence.
- 1861 taught us perspective.
- 1865 taught us strategy.
- 1896 taught us belief-driven action.

But independence has a ceiling.

At some point, self-reliance becomes self-limitation.

This is where Inflection Point 6 arrives.

It asks a question many people avoid:

> *Who am I building with—and why?*

THE FORMATION OF WEALTH COLLECTIVES

In the early 1900s, especially within communities excluded from mainstream systems, wealth did not appear through individual accumulation.

It appeared through **collective design**. This period saw the strengthening of:

- Mutual Aid Societies.
- Faith-Centered Economic Networks.
- Professional Associations.
- Historically Black Colleges And Institutions.
- Fraternal Organizations and Social Capital Systems.

These were not social clubs. They were **economic strategies**.

They existed because isolation was dangerous, and partnership was protection.

WEALTH AS A GROUP PROCESS

Here is the truth most financial advice avoids:

> *You can get rich by yourself.*
> *But to build wealth, you need people.*

People who:

- Challenge your blind spots.
- Extend your reach.
- Stabilize your risks.
- Carry the vision when you are tired.

This is not dependency.

It is design.

And it requires humility.

GETTING IN WHERE YOU FIT IN

One of the most overlooked skills in wealth-building is **placement**.

Not every room is yours.
Not every table is aligned.
Not every opportunity deserves your energy.

1909 teaches us this:

> *Belonging is strategic.*

Finding your wealth collective is not about proximity to power; it is about alignment with purpose.

Square pegs do not need to be reshaped.
They need **square holes**.

Identity matters here.

Perspective matters here.

Difference matters here.

THE FOUR PURSUITS THAT SHAPE A LIFE

At this inflection point, pursuit becomes layered.

There is:

- **The Life Pursuit.** Responding to time and chance.
- **The Lifetime Pursuit.** Enduring growth and development.
- **The Independent Pursuit.** Owning consequences.
- **The Legacy Pursuit** Confronting fear, confusion, and blind spots.

Each pursuit requires different partners.

Trying to with the same people for every pursuit creates friction.

Wisdom lies in knowing **who belongs where**.

PARTNERSHIP IS NOT PERMANENCE

Here is another critical correction.

Not all partnerships are meant to last forever.

Many are **opportunistic by design**—formed to achieve a specific outcome, then released.

This is not failure.

It is maturity.

1909 teaches us to stop romanticizing permanence and start valuing alignment.

THE EMOTIONAL COST OF GOING ALONE

Many people resist collective pursuit because it feels risky.

People disappoint.
Groups complicate.
Trust takes time.

But isolation has a cost, too.

Isolation:

- Narrows vision.
- Amplifies fear.
- Slows momentum.
- Distorts self-perception.

A wealth collective does not just expand resources.

It expands **identity**.

You begin to see yourself as others see you: capable, necessary, worthy.

DECLARATION — INFLECTION POINT 6

> *I will no longer pursue wealth alone.*
> *I will build with people aligned to my purpose.*
> *I will choose partnership over isolation.*
> *I will allow myself to be supported.*

This declaration is quiet, but it changes everything.

PRACTICE: MAPPING YOUR COLLECTIVE

Go Within.

Answer honestly:

- Who sharpens my thinking?
- Who stabilizes my risk?
- Who believes in the future I am building?
- Where am I forcing independence when partnership is required?

Write their names down.

Absence is information too.

SHARING: ENTERING THE CIRCLE

Choose one person and say:

"I am building something that requires partnership. I want to explore alignment."

Notice the response.

Alignment reveals itself quickly when named.

WHY 1909 STILL MATTERS

We live in a culture that celebrates visibility but undervalues infrastructure.

Yet history shows:

> *Movements succeed where individuals burn out.*

Collective design is not optional for enduring change.

It is essential.

CLOSING REFLECTION

Before you can build at scale...
Before you can sustain momentum...
Before you can leave a legacy...

You must answer this:

> *Who am I willing to build with—and what am I willing to contribute?*

1909 invites you to stop standing alone.

BEFORE MOVING FORWARD, NOTICE WHERE THIS INFLECTION ALREADY LIVES IN YOUR LIFE. WHAT FEELS INHERITED? WHAT FEELS CHOSEN?

EXPANSION 1916 – 1930

What are you willing to leave to become who you are?

CHAPTER 7

MIGRATION, EXPANSION, AND THE PRICE OF GROWTH

INFLECTION POINT 7: 1916–1930

WHEN STAYING BECOMES MORE DANGEROUS THAN LEAVING

There comes a moment when staying costs more than leaving.

Not emotionally—structurally.
Not symbolically—economically.
Not hypothetically—generationally.

By 1916, millions of Black Americans reached that moment.

They were no longer asking *whether* life could improve where they were.
They were asking *how long they could afford to wait*.

This is the inflection point of movement.

And movement is never neutral.

MIGRATION IS NOT ESCAPE – IT IS STRATEGY

The Great Migration is often described as a search for opportunity.

That is true, but incomplete.

Migration is not simply a pull toward something better. It is also a push away from conditions that restrict growth.

People do not uproot their lives lightly.

They move when:

- Labor is undervalued.
- Safety is conditional.
- Dignity is negotiated.
- Future generations are constrained.

Migration is a declaration that the current system cannot hold me.

EXPANSION ALWAYS HAS A PRICE

Leaving costs something.

You leave:

- Familiarity.
- Informal protection.
- Cultural fluency.
- Proximity to elders.

What you gain is not guaranteed.

You exchange known hardship for **an uncertain possibility**.

This is why Inflection Point 7 is not romantic.

It is instructional.

> *Expansion requires risk tolerance and emotional stamina.*

CARRYING CULTURE ACROSS DISTANCE

The Great Migration did not dilute culture.

It transplanted it.

Churches moved.
Music moved.
Food moved.
Entrepreneurial instincts moved.

What traveled north and west was not just labor; it was *infrastructure*.
This matters.

Because it reveals that wealth is not only built where you arrive.
It is shaped by what you carry with you.

THE DOUBLE CONSCIOUSNESS OF EXPANSION

Migration introduces duality.

You are:

- Grateful for opportunity.
- Wary of exposure.
- Hopeful for growth.
- Alert to threat.

You learn quickly that expansion does not erase differences.

It relocates it.

Opportunity exists, but so do ceilings.
Wages rise, but access is rationed.
Freedom expands, but surveillance follows.

Growth does not eliminate tension.

It relocates it to a higher level.

THE COST OF BECOMING NECESSARY

Northern industries needed labor.

They were willing to train.
They were willing to pay.
They were willing to promote, up to a point.

Being needed does not mean being equal. This is a critical wealth lesson:

> *Utility does not guarantee equity.*

Systems will take what they need from you without committing to your future.

This is why migration alone is **never** enough.

EXPANSION WITHOUT OWNERSHIP IS TEMPORARY

Migration produced income.

But income is not wealth.

Without ownership:

- Wages disappear.
- Progress resets.
- Gains are vulnerable.

This is why later inflection points will return again and again to ownership.

Migration created **space**.

But space must be claimed.

THE EMOTIONAL TAX OF GROWTH

Expansion creates grief alongside opportunity.

You grieve:

- What could not come with you?
- Who did not survive the move?
- What did safety once look like?

This grief is rarely acknowledged, but it shapes behavior.

It explains:

- Overworking.
- Hyper-independence.
- Distrust of institutions.
- Fierce loyalty to community.

Migration teaches resilience, but also caution.

WHAT THIS MEANS FOR YOU

Inflection Point 7 asks a question most people avoid:

> *Where Am I staying out of loyalty when growth requires movement?*

This is not always geographic.

It can be:

- Emotional.
- Professional.
- Relational.
- Ideological.

Staying can be wise.
Leaving can be necessary.

Discernment is the skill.

DECLARATION – INFLECTION POINT 7

> *I will move when growth requires it.*
> *I will carry my culture with intention.*
> *I will not confuse proximity with progress.*
> *I will prepare for the cost of expansion.*

This declaration does not demand speed.

It demands honesty.

PRACTICE: THE COST INVENTORY

Go Within.

Write down:

- What staying currently cost you.
- What leaving might cost you.
- What growth would require you to risk?

Do not judge the answers.

Just see them.

Clarity precedes courage.

SHARING: NAMING THE PULL

Choose one trusted person and say:

"I feel a pull toward expansion—and I'm trying to understand its cost."

Listen without defending.

Sometimes clarity arrives through witness.

WHY THIS INFLECTION STILL LIVES

We are living in another migration era.

People are moving:

- Between cities.
- Between industries.

- Between generations.
- Between belief systems.
- Between identities.

The lesson remains:

> *Movement without ownership is fragile.*
> *But stagnation without strategy is deadly.*

CLOSING REFLECTION

Before you can scale your impact...
Before you can secure your future...
Before you can claim space confidently...

You must answer this:

> *What am I willing to leave behind to grow forward?*

1916 reminds us:
Expansion is a choice and a responsibility.

BEFORE MOVING FORWARD, NOTICE WHERE THIS INFLECTION ALREADY LIVES IN YOUR LIFE. WHAT FEELS INHERITED? WHAT FEELS CHOSEN?

ACCESS — 1954

PATIENT POWER

Can you stay when the win is slow?

CHAPTER 8

EDUCATION, ACCESS, AND THE COST OF INTEGRATION

INFLECTION POINT 8: 1954

WHEN THE DOOR OPENS—BUT THE ROOM ISN'T READY YET.

1954 did not feel like victory.

It felt like tension.

Brown v. Board of Education promised access, but not belonging. It declared segregation unconstitutional, but it did not dismantle the systems that made segregation profitable, comfortable, and enforceable.

This is the lesson of Inflection Point 8:

> *Access without preparedness extracts a price.*

And someone always pays it.

EDUCATION AS THE NEW BATTLEGROUND

By the mid-20th century, it had become clear that land and labor were no longer the primary engines of American wealth.

Knowledge was.

Education determined:

- Earning potential.
- Professional access.
- Political legitimacy.
- Social mobility.

So the fight shifted.

If Black Americans could not be barred from freedom outright, they would be restricted from **preparation**.

Brown v. Board cracked that barrier.

But cracking a barrier is not the same as removing it.

INTEGRATION IS NOT ASSIMILATION

Integration was framed as progress.

But it came with a hidden expectation:

To gain access, *you must adapt*.

Adapt your speech.
Adapt your posture.
Adapt your ambition.

Integration often meant entering spaces that were not designed for you—and being evaluated by standards that ignored your context.

This is where many people learned a painful truth:

> *Access can cost you pieces of yourself if you are not anchored.*

THE UNSPOKEN TRADE-OFFS

As schools integrated:

Black teachers lost jobs.

Black institutions lost funding.

Black leadership pipelines weakened.

Progress for some came at the expense of collective infrastructure.

This is not failure, it **is unexamined trade-off**.

Inflection Point 8 teaches us that expansion without protection leads to erosion.

THE PSYCHOLOGICAL COST OF PROVING WORTH

Integration created a new pressure:

You had to be *excellent* just to be considered equal.

Mistakes were magnified.
Performance was scrutinized.
Failure felt personal and representative.

This pressure shaped generations.

It created:

- Perfectionism.
- Hyper-vigilance.
- Fear of failure.
- Chronic overperformance.

This is not resilience.

It is survival under observation.

EDUCATION BUILDS CAPACITY—BUT NOT ALWAYS POWER

Education equips individuals.

But without collective strategy, education alone does not redistribute power.

Degrees open doors.
Networks determine how far you go inside.

This is why many highly educated people still feel constrained.

They gained credentials, but not control.

WHAT THIS MEANS FOR YOU

Inflection Point 8 asks a difficult question:

> *Where have I mistaken access for alignment?*

You may have:

- Entered a system that rewards you conditionally.

- Adopted norms that conflict with your values.
- Sacrificed community for credibility.

None of this makes you wrong.

But it does require reckoning.

THE COST OF LEAVING YOUR PEOPLE BEHIND

Integration often demanded separation from familiar support systems.

To move forward, people were told—explicitly or implicitly—to move *away*.

This fractured:

- Identity.
- Loyalty.
- Shared Language.

The loss was subtle, but lasting. And it explains why so many people succeed externally while feeling internally untethered.

DECLARATION—INFLECTION POINT 8

> *I will pursue access without abandoning alignment.*
> *I will not trade my identity for opportunity.*
> *I will prepare myself for access—and protect*
> *my values within it.*

This declaration restores agency.

PRACTICE: THE ALIGNMENT AUDIT

Go Within.

Ask yourself:

- Where do I have access that costs me authenticity?
- What parts of myself have I muted to remain acceptable?
- What support systems have I neglected in pursuit of advancement?

Write it down.

Awareness is reclamation.

SHARING: NAMING THE COST

Choose one person and say:

"Gaining access has cost me something—and I'm learning how to recover it."

Let the truth breathe.

WHY 1954 STILL MATTERS

We are still negotiating integration today.

In workplaces.
In institutions.
In movements.

The lesson remains:

> *Access without strategy reproduces inequality at a higher level.*

Preparation matters.
Protection matters.
Collective memory matters.

CLOSING REFLECTION

Before you pursue the next credential...
Before you accept the next invitation...
Before you enter the next room...

You must ask:

> *What will it cost me to belong here—and is the cost worth it?*

1954 invites you to enter wisely.

BEFORE MOVING FORWARD, NOTICE WHERE THIS INFLECTION ALREADY LIVES IN YOUR LIFE. WHAT FEELS INHERITED? WHAT FEELS CHOSEN?

PROTEST 1963 — 1968

Who must gather for the dream to scale?

CHAPTER 9

MORAL AUTHORITY, PROTEST, AND THE PRICE OF VISIBILITY

INFLECTION POINT 9: 1963–1968

WHEN DIFFERENCE REFUSES TO STAY QUIET

There are moments when silence becomes impossible.

Not because people suddenly grow brave, but because the cost of invisibility becomes higher than the cost of exposure.

By 1963, America had reached such a moment.

Black Americans had migrated.
They had educated themselves.
They had integrated where allowed.

And still, the promise remained incomplete.

The contradiction was now too visible to ignore.

VISIBILITY CHANGES THE RULES

The Civil Rights Movement did not invent injustice.

It exposed it.

Television brought brutality into living rooms.
Peaceful protest revealed the cost of maintaining the status quo.
Moral clarity disrupted political convenience.

This is the central lesson of Inflection Point 9:

> *Visibility transforms private suffering into public accountability.*

But visibility is not free.

MORAL AUTHORITY IS NOT POWER—BUT IT MOVES POWER

Dr. Martin Luther King Jr. did not command armies or control capital.

What he wielded was moral authority.

Moral authority emerges when:

- Actions align with values.
- Sacrifice exposes hypocrisy.
- Restraint highlights injustice.

It unsettles systems because they cannot be easily discredited without revealing the system's internal contradiction.

This is why moral authority often triggers organized resistance.

PROTEST IS A STRATEGY, NOT A BREAKDOWN

Protest is often dismissed as disorder.

History tells a different story.

Protest is what happens when:

- Institutions fail to self-correct.
- Access remains restricted.
- Negotiation fails.

Protest is not chaos; it is **escalation**.

And escalation always carries risk.

THE PRICE OF BEING SEEN

Visibility attracts scrutiny.

Leaders became targets.
Families became vulnerable.
Communities absorbed trauma.

Dr. King, Malcolm X, Medgar Evers—visibility shortened lives.

This is the part of the story often sanitized.

> *Visibility accelerates consequence.*

It clarifies stakes.

INTERNAL CONFLICT WITHIN THE MOVEMENT

Inflection Point 9 was not unified.

There were debates:

- nonviolence vs. self-defense.
- integration vs. separation.
- moral appeal vs. political leverage.

These tensions were not weakness.

They were evidence of **maturation**.

Movements fracture when growth demands complexity.

WHAT THIS TEACHES YOU

Inflection Point 9 asks a direct question:

> *What truth am I willing to make visible,*
> *knowing it may cost me?*

Visibility today looks different.

It may be:

- Naming inequity at work.
- Setting boundaries in family.
- Speaking against consensus.
- Refusing to perform gratitude.

The stakes change, but the principle remains.

MORAL AUTHORITY BEGINS INTERNALLY

You cannot claim moral authority publicly if you are misaligned privately.

Visibility without integrity collapses.

This is why belief must drive action, and action requires ownership of position.

You cannot borrow conviction.

DECLARATION – INFLECTION POINT 9

> *I will not hide my truth to preserve comfort.*
> *I will align my actions with my values.*
> *I accept the cost of being seen.*

This declaration is not loud.

It is grounded.

PRACTICE: THE VISIBILITY THRESHOLD

Go Within.

Ask yourself:

- What truth have I kept private out of fear?
- Where have I minimized myself to avoid conflict?
- What would integrity require me to name—now?

Write it down.

Courage begins in clarity.

SHARING: SPEAKING IT ALOUD

Choose one person and say:

"There is something I've been holding back because being seen felt risky."

Do not justify.
Do not overexplain.

Visibility does its own work.

WHY 1968 STILL ECHOES

The assassination of Dr. King marked a rupture.

It revealed that moral authority threatens entrenched power.

And yet his vision persists.

Because moral authority does not die with individuals.

It transfers.

CLOSING REFLECTION

Before you pursue influence...
Before you build platforms...
Before you speak for others...

Ask yourself:

> *What am I willing to risk to live in alignment with what I believe?*

1963–1968 reminds us:

Change becomes inevitable once truth is visible.

BEFORE MOVING FORWARD, NOTICE WHERE THIS INFLECTION ALREADY LIVES IN YOUR LIFE. WHAT FEELS INHERITED? WHAT FEELS CHOSEN?

REPRESENTATION 1972 — 1980

What can rise after everthing falls?

CHAPTER 10

REPRESENTATION, POWER, AND THE LIMITS OF ACCESS

INFLECTION POINT 10: 1972–1980

WHEN THE DOOR OPENS—BUT THE BUILDING STILL ISN'T YOURS

By the early 1970s, something undeniable had happened.

Black Americans were no longer just protesting power. They were **entering it**.

Shirley Chisholm ran for president.
The Congressional Black Caucus was formed.
Black mayors were elected in major cities.
Seats at decision-making tables—long denied—were finally occupied.

And yet, a new realization emerged:

Representation is not the same as control.

This is the lesson of Inflection Point 10.

THE PROMISE—AND THE TRAP—OF REPRESENTATION

Representation matters.

It signals possibility.
It changes narratives.
It interrupts exclusion.

But representation also carries a quiet risk.

When representation is mistaken for power, people stop asking harder questions:

- Who controls the budget?
- Who sets the rules?
- Who defines success?
- Who bears the consequences when policies fail?

Visibility without leverage creates frustration.

And frustration, left unexamined, turns inward.

FROM MOVEMENT TO MANAGEMENT

I was born in 1972, old enough to remember the air of the late twentieth century, and young enough to inherit its promises as if they were permanent.

The 1970s marked a transition.

Movements give way to institutions.
Charisma gives way to bureaucracy.
Vision gives way to negotiation.

This is not corruption.

It is **complexity.**

Governance requires compromise.
Compromise exposes constraints.

Many leaders discovered that entering power meant inheriting systems designed to limit them.

THE LIMITS BECOME CLEAR

Cities led by newly elected Black officials faced:

- Shrinking tax bases.
- Federal disinvestment.
- Inherited debt.
- Rising expectations.

Representation arrived at the same time as austerity.

This is not coincidence.

It is pattern.

Access is often granted when systems are under strain—when responsibility can be transferred without resources.

WHAT THIS REVEALS ABOUT POWER

Inflection Point 10 exposes a hard truth:

> *Power is not where you sit.*
> *It is what you can change.*

Being invited into the room does not guarantee authority.

Authority flows from:

- Control of capital.
- Ownership of infrastructure.
- Ability to shape outcomes.

Without these, representation becomes symbolic.

THE EMOTIONAL WEIGHT OF "ALMOST"

This era produced a specific kind of exhaustion.

People had:

- Waited generations for access.
- Fought visibly for inclusion.
- Sacrificed deeply.

And yet, progress felt partial.

This created:

- Cynicism.
- Disengagement.
- Internal division.
- Blame within communities.

When power disappoints, people turn on each other.

THE LESSON FOR YOU

Inflection Point 10 asks a sobering question:

> *Where have I mistaken proximity to power for actual influence?*

You may have:

- The title but not the authority.
- The platform, but not the budget.
- The responsibility but not the discretion.

This is not personal failure.

It is structural reality.

And clarity is required.

RECLAIMING AGENCY WITHIN CONSTRAINTS

Understanding limits is not defeat.

It is strategy.

When you see constraints clearly, you can:

- Build parallel systems.
- Accumulate leverage.
- Invest where returns compound.
- Stop wasting energy on symbolic wins.

This is where wealth thinking matures.

DECLARATION — INFLECTION POINT 10

> *I will not confuse representation with power.*
> *I will seek leverage, not just access.*
> *I will build influence where decisions are made.*

This declaration shifts focus from visibility to impact.

PRACTICE: THE POWER AUDIT

Go Within.

Ask yourself:

- Where do I have access but limited influence?
- What decisions affect me that I do not help shape?
- Where could I build leverage instead of waiting for permission?

Write it down.

Clarity restores agency.

SHARING: NAMING THE CONSTRAINT

Choose one trusted person and say:

"I'm realizing where my influence stops, and where I need to build differently."

This is not complaint.

It is calibration.

WHY THE 1970S STILL MATTER

We live in an era obsessed with representation.

But history warns us:

> *Access without ownership leads to disappointment.*

Real change requires:

- Control.
- Continuity.
- Capital.

Anything less will cycle.

CLOSING REFLECTION

Before you accept the next role...
Before you celebrate the next milestone...
Before you mistake invitation for impact...

Ask yourself:

> *What power does this position actually give me?*

1972–1980 teaches us to look past the chair—and toward the table itself.

BEFORE MOVING FORWARD, NOTICE WHERE THIS INFLECTION ALREADY LIVES IN YOUR LIFE. WHAT FEELS INHERITED? WHAT FEELS CHOSEN?

TEST OF BELIEF 2008 — 2016

Do you believe the promise
includes you?

CHAPTER 11

CRISIS, OPPORTUNITY, AND THE TEST OF BELIEF

INFLECTION POINT 11: 2008–2016

CRISIS, OPPORTUNITY, AND THE TEST OF BELIEF

Every system eventually tests what it claims to believe.

Not with words.
With pressure.

Between 2008 and 2016, America entered one of those tests.

A financial collapse that began quietly—inside balance sheets, mortgage products, and risk models—spilled into living rooms, retirement accounts, churches, classrooms, and dinner tables. Jobs vanished. Homes disappeared. Trust evaporated.

And what many people discovered, often too late, was this:

They had access...
but not ownership.

They had participation...
but not protection.

They had been included in the economy,
but never positioned within it.

This inflection point is not about what happened *to* America.
It is about what was revealed *within* it.

And within us.

CRISIS IS A MIRROR, NOT AN ACCIDENT

Crises do not create new truths.
They **expose existing ones**.

2008 exposed:

- How risk was transferred downward.
- How profit had been privatized while loss was socialized.
- How belief in systems replaced understanding of them.

Many people believed they were building wealth.

They were not.

They were renting stability.

And when the market corrected, renters absorbed the shock.

This is not a moral judgment.
It is a structural reality.

THE HIDDEN COST OF OUTSOURCED BELIEF

Most people did what they were told.

They trusted:

- The System.

- The Professionals.
- The Institutions.
- The Narratives.

They believed participation was enough.

But belief without ownership is fragile.

And belief without agency is dangerous.

This inflection point asks a question that cannot be avoided:

> *Who were you trusting with your future—and why?*

Because belief always drives action.

And unexamined belief drives misaligned action.

OPPORTUNITY DOES NOT ANNOUNCE ITSELF LOUDLY

Here is the uncomfortable truth:

While millions were losing ground, others were positioning themselves.

During this same period:

- Assets were discounted.
- Markets reset.
- Power consolidated.
- Influence reorganized.

Crisis compressed timelines.

Those who understood cycles moved quickly.
Those who relied on stability waited for normal to return.

Normal never returns.

It only evolves.

THIS WAS THE TEST OF BELIEF

This inflection point did not ask:
Do you have money?

It asked:
Do you understand money?

It did not ask:
Are you included?

It asked:
Are you positioned?

It did not ask:
Do you believe in the system?

It asked:
Do you believe in **yourself** enough to act independently?

This is where the NarrowRoad™ narrows.

BELIEF REQUIRES OWNERSHIP OF POSITION

Along the NarrowRoad™, belief is not emotional.
It is directional.

Belief means:

- Owning your position.
- Understanding your risks.
- Naming your non-negotiables.
- Acting even when consensus hesitates.

This period separated people who believed *something would save them* from those who believed *they must build.*

That difference is everything.

THE ILLUSION OF SAFETY

One of the most dangerous beliefs exposed during this era was the belief in safety.

Safety in:

- Credentials.
- Titles.
- Salaries.
- Institutions.
- Proximity to power.

But safety that is not rooted in ownership is **temporary**.

And safety that discourages questioning eventually becomes captivity.

Crisis strips illusion.

REFLECTION: WHAT DID YOU LEARN ABOUT YOURSELF?

Ask yourself:

- Where did I freeze instead of move?
- Where did I wait for permission instead of acting?
- What beliefs did I inherit that failed me here?

This is not about shame.

It is about **clarity**.

Because clarity restores power.

THE QUIET EMERGENCE OF A NEW WEALTH BUILDER

Between 2008 and 2016, a new kind of wealth builder emerged.

Not louder.
Not flashier.
But **clearer**.

These were people who:

- Learned how systems work.
- Built parallel strategies.
- Diversified belief, not just assets.
- Invested in education, relationships, and leverage.

They stopped asking for inclusion.

They started building alternatives.

THE SPIRITUAL UNDERCURRENT

This inflection point was not only financial.

It was existential.

People questioned:

- The meaning of success.
- The cost of stability.
- The relationship between faith and fear.

Many discovered that faith without action is fragile.

And action without belief is unsustainable.

The NarrowRoad™ requires both.

DECLARATION – INFLECTION POINT 11

Write this. Say it. Own it:

> *I examine what I believe.*
> *I own my position.*
> *I act with clarity, not consensus.*

This is not rebellion.

It is responsibility.

PRACTICE: THE BELIEF AUDIT

This week:

- Identify one belief you inherited about money, success, or safety.
- Test it against your lived experience.
- Decide whether it still deserves your loyalty.

Belief must earn its place.

WHY THIS INFLECTION POINT MATTERS

If Inflection Point 1 teaches you to **see your value,**
and Inflection Point 2 teaches you to **declare independence,**

then Inflection Point 11 teaches you to **stand firm when systems shake**.

This is the test before the final turn.

Because what comes next is not survival.

It is **legacy**.

CLOSING THOUGHT

Crisis does not ask who you *say* you are.

It asks who you have prepared to be.

And preparation, along the NarrowRoad™, has always been the quiet work of belief turned into ownership.

BEFORE MOVING FORWARD, NOTICE WHERE THIS INFLECTION ALREADY LIVES IN YOUR LIFE. WHAT FEELS INHERITED? WHAT FEELS CHOSEN?

LEGACY 2017 – PRESENT

OWNERSHIP

What must be finished so others can build upon your legacy?

CHAPTER 12

CHOOSING THE LEGACY YOU WILL LEAVE

INFLECTION POINT 12: 2017–PRESENT

THE MOMENT WHERE HISTORY STOPS CARRYING YOU

Every long experiment reaches a point where momentum runs out.

Not because it failed.
But because it can no longer carry people who can no longer carry it without renegotiating its terms.

That is where we are now.

From 2017 to the present, America entered a phase that cannot be explained by economics alone, politics alone, or culture alone. What we are living through is **a reckoning of ownership**.

Not ownership of land only.
Not ownership of capital only.
But ownership of **position, belief, and responsibility**.

This is the inflection point where the question is no longer *what happened to us*, but:

> *What will we do with what we inherited?*

THE END OF INNOCENCE

Earlier inflection points allowed distance.

You could say:

That was before my time.

That was structural.

That was inevitable.

Those explanations no longer hold.

Information is available.
History is documented.
Patterns are visible.

Which means neutrality is no longer passive.

It is a choice.

And every choice carries legacy.

EXPOSURE WITHOUT INFRASTRUCTURE

This era is marked by visibility.

Everything is exposed:

- Inequity.
- Hypocrisy.

- Fragility.
- Opportunity.
- Deception.

But exposure without infrastructure creates anxiety. People can see what is broken, but they do not know where to stand. They can name injustice, but not strategy. They can demand change, but not always sustain it. This is what happens when belief outpaces structure.

THE FALSE PROMISE OF AWARENESS

Awareness is not action.
Language is not leverage.
Outrage is not ownership.

Many people believe that seeing the problem is the same as solving it.

History says otherwise.

Every inflection point that moved the wheel forward required:

- Organization.
- Sacrifice.
- Patience.
- Shared standards.

This moment is no different.

THE RETURN OF THE NARROWROAD™

The NarrowRoad™ has always been about ownership of position.

Not louder voices.
Not perfect agreement.
But clear alignment between:

- What you believe.
- How you act.
- What you are willing to carry.

This is the era where belief must be funded.

With time.
With discipline.
With relationships.
With capital.

Otherwise, belief becomes performance.

LEGACY IS NO LONGER ABSTRACT

Legacy is not what you say you stand for.

Legacy is what survives you.

It is:

- The systems you strengthen.
- The people you prepare.
- The resources you steward.
- The conflicts you resolve instead of pass on.

Inflection Point 12 reveals that legacy is not future tense.

It is **present behavior** with long consequences.

THE MYTH OF "LATER"

One of the most dangerous beliefs in this era is *later*.

Later, I'll invest.
Later, I'll organize.
Later, I'll teach my children.
Later, I'll step into leadership.

History is unforgiving with delay. Every generation that waited inherited less freedom, not more. Later is how opportunities expire quietly.

CHOOSING THE TORCH

At every previous inflection point, someone carried the torch:

- Before they were ready.
- Before conditions were ideal.
- Before consensus existed.

They were criticized.
They were doubted.
They were misunderstood.

And yet, without them, there would be no road to walk.

This is your moment to decide:

> *What torch am I carrying—and for whom?*

REFLECTION: THE OWNERSHIP QUESTION

Sit with this—not emotionally, but honestly:

- What do I fully own today?
- Where am I still renting safety?
- Who benefits from my hesitation?
- What would collapse if I stopped pretending and chose alignment?

Legacy clarity begins here.

THE WEALTH THAT LASTS

A different kind of wealth is not measured only in money.

It is measured in:

- Continuity.
- Coherence.
- Courage.
- Contribution.

Money amplifies these qualities.
It does not replace them.

Those who confuse accumulation with legacy leave volatility behind.

Those who align wealth with purpose leave infrastructure.

DECLARATION – INFLECTION POINT 12

Write this as a line in the sand:

> *I choose my legacy deliberately.*
> *I fund what I believe.*
> *I carry my difference forward for others to stand on.*

This is not pressure.

It is permission.

PRACTICE: THE LEGACY DECISION

This week, choose one action that moves you from awareness to ownership.

Not symbolic.
Not performative.
Structural.

Something that will still matter in ten years.

THE FINAL TRUTH

America has always been an experiment.

What has changed is this:

We now know the cost of avoiding responsibility.

We know what happens when ownership is deferred.
We know what happens when belief is borrowed.
We know what happens when difference is hidden instead of stewarded.

The future does not belong to the loudest voices.

It belongs to those who:

- Understand the road.
- Choose their position.
- Walk it with others.
- And leave it stronger than they found it.

CLOSING: YOUR TURN ON THE ROAD

This book cannot walk for you.

But it can tell you the truth.

You are different.
Your difference matters.
And the wheel of wealth does not turn on intention alone.

It turns when someone decides to push.

Welcome to the last inflection point.

Now choose what you will leave behind.

This book does not complete the journey. It reveals the road. What happens next—individually and collectively—depends on whether we choose to walk it together.

BEFORE MOVING FORWARD, NOTICE WHERE THIS INFLECTION ALREADY LIVES IN YOUR LIFE. WHAT FEELS INHERITED? WHAT FEELS CHOSEN?

THE 12 INFLECTION POINTS

Each inflection point has one primary word and one activating phrase.
The single word is what lives on the tile.
The phrase is what lives in the chapter + workbook.

Together, these read like a sentence of formation:

> *Value → Freedom → Perspective → Pivot → Pursuit → Partner → Migration → Patient Power → Alliance → Resurrection → Audacity → Ownership*

That arc alone tells the story.

THE ARC BECOMES A MAP

Each inflection point joins a timeline. The timeline builds an arc.
Navigating the arc forms a road map to your difference.

Inflection Point	The Timeline	That arc tells the story.	The arc becomes a map
1 VALUE	1619	Human worth is defined, denied, and contested.	Know what you are worth.
2 FREEDOM	1776	Freedom appears as both promise and demand.	Choose what freedom requires.
3 PERSPECTIVE	1861–1865	Conflict changes what we are able to see.	See differently.
4 PIVOT	1865	Liberation opens the need for a new direction.	Turn with intention.
5 PURSUIT	1896	Change asks what you are willing to pursue.	Move toward what matters.
6 PARTNER	1909	Possibility expands through partnership.	Build with others.
7 MIGRATION	1939	Movement carries people toward possibility.	Go where possibility opens.
8 PATIENT POWER	1954	Persistence turns resistance into progress.	Stay the course.
9 ALLIANCE	1963	Collective belief gathers strength.	Gather collective strength.
10 RESURRECTION	1968	Interrupted dreams test what survives.	Rise after interruption.
11 AUDACITY	2009–2017	History stretches what seems possible.	Imagine beyond precedent.
12 OWNERSHIP	2019–Present	Ownership asks what we are prepared to build.	Take possession.

YOUR DIFFERENCE

Navigating the arc forms a road map to your difference.

HISTORICAL CONTEXT ADDENDUM

A companion for those who want the story behind the story. My history addendum has a name. It is called **Context**.

Because history is not just what happened. It is what happened *to you*, even if you didn't know it at the time. It is the invisible curriculum running under your life: what you were taught to expect, what you were taught to fear, what you were taught to call "normal."

Some readers grew up with this timeline in the air. Others did not. But either way, you have been breathing it.

This addendum is here to make you aware. It's orientation. "Awareness is the beginning of ownership."

The chapters you just read are not asking you to become someone new. They are asking you to **take full possession of who you already** are by understanding the inheritance you carry: culture, faith, fear, ambition, memory, and the rules you absorbed without consent.

And because America does not distribute inheritance equally, it also does not distribute wealth equally, at least not the kind that lasts. That is one of the ways we are different.

So we are going to walk through the **twelve inflection points**: moments where belief, action, and collective consequence intersect. You are not asked to agree with every interpretation. You are asked to locate yourself inside the picture they form. Along the NarrowRoad™ seeing is believing and it is belief that drives action.

HISTORY REVEALS PATTERNS OF DIFFERENCE HIDDEN IN PLAIN SIGHT.

The book *The Fourth Turning* impacted me and my work almost twenty years ago because it helped me to see the pattern within history. *The Fourth Turning* is not a fortune-teller; it is a pattern reader. It reminds us that history moves in recognizable cycles of disruption, rebuilding, and renewal, cycles people rarely recognize while they are inside them.

This addendum is the context layer. Each inflection point names what was in the air, what changed, and what it produced, so you can "read the room" of American history; what it believed, what it protected, what it denied, and what it built anyway. When you understand the pattern, your difference stops being a burden and becomes leverage. Context does not trap you; it trains you. And once you can see the wheel turning, you can push it forward with intention. That is how history, once understood, can become a culturally relevant prophecy.

Before we begin, one lens really matters.

EPIGRAPH LENS (THE 400-YEAR FRAME)

The Book of Genesis doesn't treat time like trivia. It treats time like an accounting period.

"...For four hundred years your descendants will be strangers in a country not their own, and that they will be enslaved and mistreated there...and in the end they will come away with great wealth." Genesis 15: 13-15

Scripture treats time like a sentence with consequences.

So does history.

This addendum uses that same logic: duration produces outcomes, and history leaves receipts. Looking through time from this biblical lens reveals a new pattern is forming. Its time for everyone to come away with their different kind of wealth.

HOW TO LEARN FROM EACH INFLECTION POINT LENS

Each inflection point includes:

- **Context** (what was happening).
- **Who led the era** (presidential frame when relevant).
- **Policies + power moves** (the rules that changed outcomes).
- **Middle-class snapshot** (what "normal" looked like—and for whom).
- **Wealth vehicles** (the tools available to build/keep wealth).
- **Cross-community milestones** (so "America" means *all* of America).
- **Wealth insight** (your "different" conclusion).
- **Mantra** (your line that turns history into action).

INFLECTION POINT 1: VALUE – 1619 (JAMESTOWN)

"SEE YOUR VALUE."

THE HEADWIND

The time is 1619, and America is still in its pre-nation stage. It's an economy looking for a model, a colony looking for profit, a society deciding what it will normalize. Before there are stock exchanges or retirement accounts, there is valuation: who is protected by law, who is priced by power, and who is denied the right to own what they produce.

LEADERSHIP CONTEXT

- President(s): Not applicable (pre-U.S. presidency).
- National posture: colonial expansion; wealth formation through land and labor control.

BRIEFING

- **What's happening:** colonial economies expand through agriculture, trade, and forced labor.

- **What shifts structurally:** the earliest wealth **infrastructure** becomes racialized; ownership, rights, and protection begin to travel together.

POWER & POLICY SIGNALS

- Colonial charters and local legal systems begin **formalizing** property, labor hierarchy, and enforceable status.

MIDDLE-CLASS SNAPSHOT

- No modern middle class; social position is shaped by land, trade roles, servitude, and proximity to power.

WEALTH VEHICLES

- Land grants and land accumulation.
- Trade monopolies and merchant networks.
- Inheritance rules and family claims.
- Labor extraction as the compounding engine.

MILESTONES ACROSS COMMUNITIES (SELECTED)

- **Black communities:** enslaved Africans create **uncompensated** agricultural and trade wealth that becomes the financial backbone of the colonies and early U.S. economy, establishing a racialized wealth hierarchy. [1][2]
- **White communities:** white planters and merchants **consolidate** land, labor control, and early capital advantages (land grants, trading rights), embedding intergenerational wealth advantages. [2][1]

DOCUMENTED BREAKTHROUGHS: WHO MOVED THE WHEEL

- The "breakthrough" here is structural: an economy learns to convert people into property and call it lawful—and that architecture compounds. [1][2]

OUR INHERITANCE

1) VALUE – 1619

America learned early that wealth can be built through systems—law, labor, land, and inheritance—that decide how value is recognized and rewarded. That's the national inflection: value is not only personal; it is also institutional shaped by what a society measures, protects, and passes down.

Many of us inherit echoes of that structure in quieter forms: standards we didn't set, assumptions that precede us, and measurements that don't always reflect our full worth. Sometimes the gap is subtle—what gets praised versus what gets promoted, what gets tolerated versus what gets trusted. Your work is to name your value with clarity—so your choices, boundaries, and building strategy come from a definition of worth you can live with.

This is why difference matters: it helps you notice when a standard is too small for who you are. When you can see that clearly, you stop building for external approval and start building from self-definition—the kind that holds under pressure.

YOUR WORK (REFLECTION)

Where is your difference trying to tell you the truth?

I'm noticing: ________________________________

I'm naming: ________________________________

I'm choosing: ________________________________

Bonus prompt: What part of your value have you been leaving "unclaimed" because it wasn't recognized in the room you were in?

INFLECTION POINT 2: FREEDOM—1776

"CHART YOUR OWN PATH."

THE HEADWIND

The time is 1776, and America is in its emergent stages, more declaration than infrastructure. The words are sweeping: liberty, independence, self-rule. But the nation has not yet built the machinery that makes liberty durable or decided who fully belongs inside its promise.

LEADERSHIP CONTEXT

- President(s): Not yet (first U.S. president takes office in 1789).
- National posture: nation-building; rights language rising faster than rights enforcement.

BRIEFING

- What's happening: independence is declared; institutions are being designed.
- What shifts structurally: freedom becomes a national organizing story, but wealth outcomes will be shaped

by law, property protection, and access to emerging financial systems.

POWER & POLICY SIGNALS

- New governance structures begin forming—courts, taxation, enforcement, and finance, creating the machinery that converts ideals into outcomes.

MIDDLE-CLASS SNAPSHOT

- The middle class is not yet fully formed; households are primarily agrarian or trades-based, with status tied to land and legal recognition.

WEALTH VEHICLES

- Land ownership.
- Early banking and credit relationships.
- Government finance and institutional capital formation.
- Small enterprise ownership.

MILESTONES ACROSS COMMUNITIES (SELECTED)

- **White communities:** independence secures political power and property rights for white male landowners, protecting accumulated colonial wealth through law and new financial institutions. [3][2]
- **Black communities:** free Black communities in Northern cities slowly emerge, with some artisans and sailors earning wages and purchasing property despite slavery's expansion elsewhere. [4][2]

DOCUMENTED BREAKTHROUGHS: WHO MOVED THE WHEEL

- Independence establishes the right to set terms: rules around property, protection, and participation that shape who can compound wealth. [3][2]

OUR INHERITANCE

In 1776, America declares independence before it has a fully formed model for how freedom would be administered, financed, and protected. That's the national inflection: ideals can be announced quickly, but lived freedom requires systems, rules, responsibilities, and institutions that make liberty workable.

Many of us inherit this privately: we can name what we want, but we still have to build the capacity that makes it real—skills, habits, protections, and support. It's the difference between wanting room and having a plan for what to do with it. Your work is to chart your path with conviction and design, so freedom becomes practical, not only inspirational.

This is why difference matters: it helps you separate language from lived reality. When you can tell the difference, you stop treating freedom as a feeling and start treating it as architecture.

YOUR WORK (REFLECTION)

Where is your difference trying to tell you the truth?

I'm noticing: ______________________________

I'm naming: ______________________________

I'm choosing: ______________________________

INFLECTION POINT 3: PERSPECTIVE — 1861-1865 (CIVIL WAR)

"STORM TO FORM."

THE HEADWIND

The time is 1861–1865, and America is no longer debating in theory. The nation is splitting over power, labor, and the meaning of human value—over whether a country can call itself free while running a wealth engine built on bondage. This is what it looks like when a contradiction becomes too expensive to maintain.

LEADERSHIP CONTEXT

- **President(s):** Abraham Lincoln.
- **National posture:** rupture, mobilization, and a forced confrontation with the nation's economic and moral architecture.

BRIEFING

- **What's happening:** the Union fractures; war accelerates industrial production and financial capacity in the North.
- **What shifts structurally:** emancipation ends chattel slavery—transforming what had been treated as property

into the possibility (not the guarantee) of wages, ownership, and mobility.

POWER & POLICY SIGNALS

- Wartime governance expands federal power and the reach of national policy.
- Emancipation is introduced as national policy during the war, changing what the economy can legally defend. [5][2]

MIDDLE-CLASS SNAPSHOT

- The economy is divided: industrial North, plantation South.
- Wartime finance, contracts, and rail expansion deepen Northern capital markets.

WEALTH VEHICLES

- Wartime finance and government contracts.
- Industrial expansion and railroads.
- Banking growth and deepening capital markets.

MILESTONES ACROSS COMMUNITIES (SELECTED)

- **Black communities:** emancipation ends chattel slavery, converting a system where Black people were held as property into the potential for wage-earning and ownership—opening the door (though not guaranteeing) mobility. [5][2]
- **White communities:** wartime finance, industrial contracts, and railroad expansion grow Northern wealth and deepen capital markets that others will later have to navigate. [2][3]

DOCUMENTED BREAKTHROUGHS: WHO MOVED THE WHEEL

- Emancipation functions as a structural break—changing what the nation can legally treat as an asset and who can claim the fruit of their labor. [5][2]

OUR INHERITANCE

The country discovered that conflict reveals what a nation actually values and what it is willing to restructure. The Civil War clarified the cost of unresolved contradictions and the price of postponing hard decisions. That's the national inflection: pressure exposes the architecture beneath the story.

Many of us inherit a version of this: seasons that test our assumptions and show us what is stable, what is fragile, and what was never truly supported. A crisis does not create character so much as it reveals what was already carrying the load. Your work is to keep perspective under pressure—so you can make decisions rooted in reality, not reaction.

This is why difference matters: it strengthens discernment when circumstances get loud. It helps you separate what is urgent from what is important, so you can build forward rather than bounce back.

YOUR WORK (REFLECTION)

Where is your difference trying to tell you the truth?

I'm noticing: ______________________________

I'm naming: ______________________________

I'm choosing: ______________________________

INFLECTION POINT 4:
PIVOT – 1865 (RECONSTRUCTION)
"REBUILD WITH INTENTION."

THE HEADWIND

The time is 1865–1895, and America is standing in the "after." The war is over, but the argument has simply changed form. Reconstruction is a contested rebuilding—one of the clearest examples of how a nation can announce a new reality while quietly restoring the old one through different tools.

LEADERSHIP CONTEXT

- **President(s):** Andrew Johnson → Ulysses S. Grant (and the drift through late-19th-century leadership).
- **National posture:** rebuilding, backlash, and uneven enforcement.

BRIEFING

- **What's happening:** political participation expands; schools and institutions are built; Black land ownership begins to emerge—then faces organized restriction.
- **What shifts structurally:** rights expand on paper, but protection and enforcement become inconsistent,

creating a recurring American pattern: "legal" does not automatically mean "protected."

POWER & POLICY SIGNALS

- Reconstruction-era reforms expand citizenship and political participation; backlash hardens through local control and Jim Crow architecture. [6][1][2]

MIDDLE-CLASS SNAPSHOT

- Industrialization accelerates; wage labor and urban markets expand.
- For many freed households, limited access to land, credit, and legal protection constrains durable asset growth.

WEALTH VEHICLES

- Land ownership and small enterprise (opportunities unevenly distributed).
- Education and institution-building as wealth infrastructure.
- Railroads, banking, and industrial investment as dominant engines.

MILESTONES ACROSS COMMUNITIES (SELECTED)

- **Black communities:** Freedmen's Bureau schools, political officeholding, and land purchases create early Black landowners, professionals, and savers, with Black wealth growing faster than white wealth from 1860s baselines. [3][5][2]
- **White communities:** white capital reasserts control through railroads, banking, and Jim Crow laws,

maintaining a large racial wealth gap even as some Black families gain assets. [6][1][2]

DOCUMENTED BREAKTHROUGHS: WHO MOVED THE WHEEL

- Reconstruction institution-building (schools, civic participation, land attempts) becomes a foundational model of building under pressure—and a warning about what happens when enforcement is withdrawn. [6][3][2]

OUR INHERITANCE

America learned that change can be announced and still require protection to endure. Reconstruction showed that progress needs structure—clarity, enforcement, and durability—if it is going to last. That's the national inflection: rebuilding is not a moment; it is a method.

Many of us inherit the experience of uneven progress: doors that open, pathways that remain complicated, gains that require steady attention. Freedom can be declared while access remains conditional, and opportunity can be promised while accountability stays inconsistent. Your work is to rebuild with intention—document what matters, create safeguards, and design for durability so what you build can be kept and grown.

This is why difference matters: it helps you plan for longevity instead of living on optimism. It turns your awareness into strategy—so progress becomes something you can hold, not just something you can name.

YOUR WORK (REFLECTION)

Where is your difference trying to tell you the truth?

I'm noticing: ______________________________

I'm naming: ______________________________

I'm choosing: ______________________________

INFLECTION POINT 5: PURSUIT 1896

"BUILD YOUR STANDARD."

OPENING SCENE

The time is 1896, and America is modernizing at full speed—industry scaling, cities swelling, fortunes consolidating. But modernization does not automatically produce fairness. Wealth is becoming national in scale, and the country is negotiating what kind of nation it will be when money, law, and power start traveling together as a system.

This is a standard-setting era—because the country begins codifying "order" in ways that look civilized while quietly sorting people into different futures. Standards are being set—some in law, some in custom, some in the fine print of who gets access and who gets delayed. And once those rules harden, they don't just shape behavior. They shape inheritance.

LEADERSHIP CONTEXT

- **President(s):** Grover Cleveland (until 1897) → William McKinley (1897–1901).

- **National posture:** consolidation, expansion, industrial scale, and a rising tension between monopoly power and public legitimacy, which leads to the hardening of social boundaries through policy and practice.

BRIEFING

- **What's happening:** segregation is formalized; the country's "rules" and "norms" begin aligning to produce predictable separation in opportunity. [4][6]
- **What shifts structurally:** exclusion becomes less "personal" and more procedural—built into systems that can call themselves neutral while producing predictable outcomes embedded in schools, work, housing, and credit access.

POWER & POLICY SIGNALS

- Plessy v. Ferguson (1896) legitimizes "separate but equal," shaping education, public access, and the rules beneath opportunity. [4][3]
- Local and state policy begins building a durable segregation architecture that reaches into labor markets and lending norms. [6][1][2]

MIDDLE-CLASS SNAPSHOT

- The middle class is becoming more recognizable through wage labor, unions, and urban professions—though access to those ladders is uneven.
- "Normal" begins to mean: stable work, a household economy, and the hope of upward mobility—often gated by race, location, and legal standing.

WEALTH VEHICLES

- Corporate equity and industrial ownership dominate elite wealth.
- Banking and insurance deepen as institutional tools of stability and leverage.
- Real estate becomes a more formalized store of value as cities expand.

MILESTONES ACROSS COMMUNITIES (SELECTED)

- **Black communities:** standards become a survival strategy—excellence, institutions, and long-game planning in a system designed to limit outcomes.
- **White communities:** industrial and professional pathways expand access to capital and institutional influence.
- **Immigrant communities:** enterprise networks grow in urban corridors, creating pathways from labor to ownership for some.
- **System note:** this era teaches a quiet truth—rules that claim neutrality can still be built to exclude.

DOCUMENTED BREAKTHROUGHS: WHO MOVED THE WHEEL)

- Plessy (1896) becomes a century-defining "standard" that reshapes education, housing, work, and public space—until later dismantled through strategic legal effort. [4][6].

INHERITANCE

In 1896, America entered a standard-setting era—where law and custom helped define who would have access and on what terms. That's the national inflection: standards don't only describe a society; they shape outcomes, and then those outcomes start to look "normal."

Many of us inherit standards we didn't design, along with the subtle pressure to confuse compliance with progress. We learn what gets rewarded and what gets delayed, what feels "reasonable" and what gets labeled "too much." Your work is to build a standard you believe in—one that protects your future, clarifies your boundaries, and guides what you will and will not normalize.

This is why difference matters: it alerts you to misalignment early—before you internalize it. When you can see a standard clearly, you can decide whether to adopt it, adapt it, or build a better one.

YOUR WORK (REFLECTION)

Where is your difference trying to tell you the truth?

I'm noticing: ______________________________

I'm naming: ______________________________

I'm choosing: ______________________________

INFLECTION POINT 6: PARTNER 1909

"FIND YOUR PEOPLE."

OPENING SCENE

The time is 1909, and America is shifting from individual wealth to institutional power. The country is scaling everything—industry, cities, finance, politics, and public life. Wealth is increasingly negotiated through organizations—banks, courts, universities, corporations, and civic movements. In this kind of economy, talent still matters, but infrastructure decides what scales.

In a world built on institutions, isolation is not just lonely—it's expensive. This is the era when "who you are with" becomes part of what you can become. The quiet lesson of the era is that isolation has a cost—because systems reward networks, coordinated strategy, and durable institutions.

LEADERSHIP CONTEXT

- **President(s):** William Howard Taft (1909–1913).
- **National posture:** Progressive reforms, trust-busting energy, expanding civic organization, and public pressure

for institutional guardrails, and a contest over how much the public should restrain private power.

BRIEFING

- **What's happening:** corporations and banks expand influence; reformers push regulation; social movements and professional associations grow.
- **What shifts structurally:** belonging becomes economic wealth, which becomes increasingly mediated through organizations—corporations, courts, universities, foundations, and networks.

POWER & POLICY SIGNALS

- Antitrust enforcement and regulatory debates expand (the public begins demanding guardrails). Progressive Era reforms shape labor, regulation, and business norms—often centering those already positioned for access. [3][2]
- Professionalization grows—credentials and institutional access become wealth infrastructure. Formal organizations become vehicles through which rights, jobs, and legitimacy are negotiated.

MIDDLE-CLASS SNAPSHOT

- Urban jobs and professions expand; professional pathways become more defined; and education becomes a stronger pathway into stability.
- Networks become a quiet divider: the same city can hold multiple "economies" depending on who can access

institutions. The middle class increasingly depends on institutional access: credentials, networks, and protected pathways.

WEALTH VEHICLES

- Banking and insurance deepen; corporate equity is an elite engine.
- Professional credentials become wealth infrastructure.
- Institutional philanthropy begins to formalize in ways that shape public life (a precursor to later "legitimacy philanthropy" patterns).

MILESTONES ACROSS COMMUNITIES (SELECTED)

- **Black communities:** the founding of the NAACP and related efforts build legal and political infrastructure to challenge exclusion, laying the groundwork for future access to jobs, housing, and capital. [2][3][4]
- **White communities:** many Progressive reforms disproportionately benefit white workers and entrepreneurs, accelerating broader white middle-class asset building. [3][2]
- **Latino communities:** early 20th-century labor demand expands participation in agriculture and industry; community networks and mutual aid begin functioning as economic stability strategies in key regions.
- **Asian American communities:** despite exclusion laws, small merchant families and farmers establish niches in West Coast agriculture and local trade, seeding future wealth pathways. [7]

- **Indigenous nations / Tribal nations:** sovereignty and land pressures continue; access to institutional capital and protected property rights remains constrained by federal policy and enforcement patterns.
- **System note:** this is an era when organizations become a wealth tool—because institutions determine who gets protected, financed, and recognized.

DOCUMENTED BREAKTHROUGHS: WHO MOVED THE WHEEL

- The NAACP (1909) marks a strategic turn toward coordinated legal and civic infrastructure as a lever for economic and social access. [2][3][4]
- Charles Hamilton Houston becomes a prototype of strategic institutional power: elite legal training deployed as a long-game blueprint that helped dismantle Jim Crow through litigation strategy.

OUR INHERITANCE

In 1909, America is learning that systems don't change because someone is right. They change because someone is organized, and that belonging can function like a form of capital. That's the national inflection: institutions are where the future gets negotiated.

Most of us inherit a version of this in private: either we build alone and wonder why progress stalls, or we build in community and watch outcomes scale. Your work is to choose partnership intentionally—not as a social preference, but as a wealth strategy. Find your people and build with them—shared standards, shared protection, shared scale—so your difference becomes leverage instead of a weight.

This is why difference matters: it helps you choose the right people and the right structures. It turns connection into strategy—so your difference becomes contribution, not complication. History, once understood, can become prophecy—because your people become the mechanism that moves the wheel.

YOUR WORK (REFLECTION)

Where is your difference trying to tell you the truth?

I'm noticing: ______________________________

I'm naming: ______________________________

I'm choosing: ______________________________

Bonus prompt: Who is one person or group you trust enough to build with—and what would "shared standards" look like in practice?

____

____

____

____

____

____

____

INFLECTION POINT 7: MIGRATION – 1939

"GO WHERE GROWTH CALLS."

THE HEADWIND

The time is 1939, and America is running on two tracks at once: recovery and mobilization. The Great Depression has reshaped what people believe about work, government, and stability. War is gathering on the horizon, and industrial demand is beginning to reorganize the map of opportunity. In that atmosphere, migration isn't just movement–it's strategy. People move toward wages, toward unions, toward safer ground, toward the kind of "normal" that can finally hold.

LEADERSHIP CONTEXT

- **President(s):** Franklin D. Roosevelt.
- **National posture:** New Deal governance, industrial mobilization, and the early architecture of a modern middle class.

BRIEFING

- **What's happening:** millions relocate for industrial jobs and wartime demand; labor markets and cities transform; household stability becomes tied to wages and policy.
- **What shifts structurally:** geography becomes a wealth variable—where you live begins to determine whether you can access the ladders that compound (jobs, benefits, homeownership, education).

POWER & POLICY SIGNALS

- New Deal-era programs expand federal involvement in banking stability, labor protections, and social safety nets—creating new pathways to stability for some households while leaving gaps for others. [2][3]
- Wartime mobilization increases industrial employment and strengthens organized labor in key sectors, changing wage dynamics and access to benefits. [4][2][3]

MIDDLE-CLASS SNAPSHOT

- "Middle class" starts to look like steady wages, benefits, and the possibility of owning a home.
- The ladders exist—but access to them is uneven by region, job type, and institutional treatment.

WEALTH VEHICLES

- Stable wage work (often tied to unions and wartime production) begins functioning like a wealth platform.

- Household saving and homeownership become more central aspirations as policy and labor markets evolve.
- Geographic mobility becomes an "invisible" wealth tool: relocating to opportunity corridors changes what a household can accumulate over time.

MILESTONES ACROSS COMMUNITIES (SELECTED)

- **Black communities:** the Great Migration moves millions from Southern sharecropping into Northern and Western industrial jobs, increasing wages, union access, and the possibility of homeownership for some families. [4][2][3]
- **Latino communities:** early waves of Mexican and other Latino workers expand across agriculture and wartime industry, gaining steadier earnings and remittance capacity that begins modest asset building. [8][9]
- **White communities:** white workers benefit disproportionately from New Deal program design and later postwar access pathways, accelerating homeownership and suburban wealth accumulation. [2][3]
- **Asian American communities:** pathways remain constrained by exclusion-era legacies and regional barriers, but family enterprise and labor participation continue to seed future upward mobility in select corridors. [7][10]
- **Indigenous nations / Tribal nations:** economic opportunity is still shaped by federal policy, land constraints, and limited access to mainstream credit and property protections—creating uneven asset pathways even as the national economy reorganizes. [2][3]

- **System note:** when opportunity moves, inequality doesn't disappear—it relocates. The question becomes who has the permission, protection, and information to move with it.

DOCUMENTED BREAKTHROUGHS: WHO MOVED THE WHEEL

- The Great Migration (as a mass household strategy) reframes mobility as an economic lever, not merely a cultural event. [4][2][3]
- New Deal labor and banking architecture establishes the idea that policy can widen stability—but design determines who gets full access. [2][3]

OUR INHERITANCE

In 1939, America is learning that opportunity does not stay put. It moves—through policy, through industry, through war, through wages, through the corridors where work becomes stable enough to compound. That's the national inflection: geography becomes part of the wealth equation, and the future is negotiated not only by what you know, but by where you can position yourself to use it.

Most of us inherit a version of this in private: either we stay loyal to terrain that cannot hold our growth, or we move toward the places and pathways where stability becomes possible. Your work is to treat movement as strategy—not as restlessness, but as stewardship. Go where growth calls. Bring what matters with you. Choose moves that increase protection, capacity, and options, so your difference becomes discernment instead of doubt.

Difference matters here because it helps you see what others sentimentalize: staying is not always faithfulness; sometimes it is limitation dressed as loyalty. And once you can tell the difference, you can move with intention. History, once understood, can become prophecy—because the right movement at the right time changes what your household can inherit.

YOUR WORK (REFLECTION)

Where is your difference trying to tell you the truth?

I'm noticing: ______________________________

I'm naming: ______________________________

I'm choosing: ______________________________

Bonus prompt: What move would increase your options one year from now—even if it feels inconvenient this month?

INFLECTION POINT 8: PATIENT POWER – 1954

"STAY THE COURSE."

THE HEADWIND

The time is 1954, and America is living inside a contradiction it can no longer keep pretending is harmless. The country is prosperous on the surface—postwar expansion, suburban growth, a widening idea of "the middle class." But the rules underneath prosperity are unevenly applied. This is the era when patience becomes power—not passive patience, but the kind that holds a line long enough for outcomes to catch up to belief.

LEADERSHIP CONTEXT

- **President(s):** Dwight D. Eisenhower.
- **National posture:** postwar expansion, institutional growth, and rising pressure on segregation-era systems.

BRIEFING

- **What's happening:** legal challenges to segregation intensify; civil rights victories begin reshaping long-term access to education, employment, and housing.
- **What shifts structurally:** the country starts weakening the legal scaffolding that protected discrimination, while wealth-building systems (home equity, job ladders, credit access) are already compounding for many households.

POWER & POLICY SIGNALS

- Brown v. Board of Education (1954) struck at the legal foundation of school segregation, setting a precedent for dismantling formal discrimination over time. [5][4][2]
- Postwar programs and institutional labor markets continue expanding opportunity, though access remains uneven by design and enforcement. [2][3]

MIDDLE-CLASS SNAPSHOT

- The postwar "middle class" increasingly means stable wages, employer benefits, and suburban homeownership—plus the expectation that each generation will do better.
- Opportunity is widening, but not evenly distributed; gaps persist in who can access appreciating neighborhoods and protected credit.

WEALTH VEHICLES

- Home equity becomes a dominant middle-class engine as suburbanization expands.

- Employer-based benefits and career ladders (especially public sector and large institutions) become stability platforms.
- Broader participation in stock ownership grows over time, layered on top of earlier access advantages.
- Education becomes a more explicit wealth pathway as credentialed work expands.

MILESTONES ACROSS COMMUNITIES (SELECTED)

- **Black communities:** Brown and related legal victories begin dismantling formal barriers, improving long-run access to higher income and wealth-building institutions—though implementation is slow and contested. [5][4][2]
- **White communities:** many families leverage earlier advantages plus postwar programs to deepen suburban home equity and increase participation in institutional wealth-building, widening gaps even as legal segregation is challenged. [3][2]
- **Latino communities:** postwar labor demand expands participation in urban and industrial work; early groundwork forms for educational and earnings gains among U.S.-born children as cities and institutions grow. [10][8][9]
- **Asian American communities:** increasing postwar labor demand and shifting pathways into education and skilled work begin compounding for U.S.-born generations, even amid continued exclusion legacies. [10][7]
- **Indigenous nations / Tribal nations:** many communities face persistent constraints tied to land, policy, and uneven access to mainstream credit systems—shaping

who can translate work into durable assets during the boom. [2][3]

- **System note:** when wealth vehicles compound over decades, timing matters—being late to access can cost more than most people realize.

DOCUMENTED BREAKTHROUGHS: WHO MOVED THE WHEEL

- Brown v. Board of Education (1954) becomes a legal inflection point—weakening the doctrine that institutionalized separate systems and widening the long-run possibility of access. [5][4][2]

OUR INHERITANCE

In 1954, America is learning that structural change often arrives through persistence over time—legal shifts, institutional shifts, cultural shifts that compound. That's the national inflection: progress can be slow and still be real, because the timeline of justice and the timeline of outcomes are rarely identical.

Most of us inherit a version of this in private: we want results quickly, but the most durable wealth outcomes often require consistency—education decisions, home decisions, career decisions, group decisions—made long before the payoff is visible. Your work is to stay the course with intelligence: making consistent decisions that compound, even when the payoff isn't immediate. This allows you to keep building capacity and to opt out of the temptation to quit simply because the timeline is longer than your emotions prefer.

Difference matters here because it trains long vision. It helps you recognize that delay is not denial—and that the people who win over decades are rarely the loudest; they are the most consistent. History, once understood, can become prophecy—because patient power turns time into an ally.

YOUR WORK (REFLECTION)

Where is your difference trying to tell you the truth?

I'm noticing: ______________________________

I'm naming: ______________________________

I'm choosing: ______________________________

BEYOND THE BINARY: THE SHARED LEGACY OF BEING 'DIFFERENT' IN A MAJORITY-RUN ENTERPRISE

The binary story—Black and White—can be true and still be incomplete.

When you tie the history of Filipino American farmworkers in California to the history of African American sharecroppers in Mississippi, you see something America rarely admits out loud: the field operations of the economy often repeat themselves. Different geography. Different language. Familiar conditions. Labor extracted. Mobility constrained. Dignity negotiated.

And when you look through the lens of business—ownership, access, credit, protection—you begin to see that patterns commonly attributed to one "racial story" show up across the historical legacies of Tribal nations, Mexican and Latino communities, and Asian American communities as well.

There is no single "model minority."
There is a shared legacy of being a minority inside a majority-run enterprise called America.

And that shared legacy matters now, because the country we are rebuilding will reward the communities that understand how to convert difference into strategy, coalition, and durable ownership.

For more on these histories and concepts, see Philip Vera Cruz's oral history of Filipino farmworkers; scholarship on the Black–white racial binary; and critiques of the 'model minority' myth.

INFLECTION POINT 9: ALLIANCE – 1963

"GATHER FOR SCALE."

THE HEADWIND

The time is 1963, and America is learning that moral clarity without coordination can still leave outcomes unchanged. The country is prosperous enough to claim progress, yet divided enough to require pressure. This is an era when the nation begins to understand something it would rather avoid: durable change usually arrives through alliances—coalitions built across organizations, faith, labor, student movements, and communities willing to carry a common demand.

LEADERSHIP CONTEXT

- **President(s):** John F. Kennedy (to Nov. 1963) → Lyndon B. Johnson (from Nov. 1963).
- **National posture:** rising civil rights urgency; federal government pulled toward legislative action.

BRIEFING

- **What's happening:** coalition-building accelerates, pushing civil rights and economic inclusion into the center of national politics.

- **What shifts structurally:** the country moves from isolated claims of injustice to coordinated demands for national policy—because scale is the only language systems reliably understand.

POWER & POLICY SIGNALS

- March on Washington for Jobs and Freedom (Aug. 28, 1963) demonstrates mass coalition power and pressures federal action.
- The march explicitly ties civil rights to jobs and economic conditions, not only social recognition.
- Momentum from this alliance era contributes to the passage of major civil rights legislation soon after (Civil Rights Act of 1964; Voting Rights Act of 1965).

MIDDLE-CLASS SNAPSHOT

- The "middle class" is increasingly defined by stable employment, benefits, and access to appreciating neighborhoods—yet neighborhoods and schools are still unequal engines.
- Institutional pathways (government, unions, credentialed professions) become the most reliable ladders into stability.

WEALTH VEHICLES

- Protected employment ladders (public sector + large institutions) increasingly function as wealth infrastructure through steady income and benefits.
- Home equity continues compounding—making fair access to housing and credit an economic issue, not just a moral one.

- Education access becomes an increasingly decisive gateway into credentialed stability.

MILESTONES ACROSS COMMUNITIES (SELECTED)

- **Black communities:** coalition-building and civil rights organizing drive expanded access to public employment, professional roles, and fairer treatment in housing and credit over time.
- **White communities:** many families retain existing wealth advantages—especially home equity in appreciating neighborhoods—even as anti-discrimination laws advance.
- **Latino communities:** civil rights reforms and immigration policy changes in the mid-1960s opened additional pathways for mobility for some segments, reshaping future labor markets and professional entry.
- **Asian American communities:** reforms that follow this era broaden skilled and family-based migration pathways for some groups, accelerating professional-class entry in later decades.
- **Indigenous nations / Tribal nations:** sovereignty and resource control remain central constraints and leverage points; alliances matter when negotiating federal recognition, rights, and durable investment into community systems.
- **System note:** alliances don't erase differences—they coordinate differences toward outcomes that no single group can secure alone.

DOCUMENTED BREAKTHROUGHS: WHO MOVED THE WHEEL

- March on Washington (Aug. 28, 1963)—a quarter million people, intentionally organized, demonstrating the power of coalition at a national scale.
- James Baldwin, *The Fire Next Time* (1963)—a cultural marker that helped clarify the moral stakes of the moment and shaped national consciousness.

OUR INHERITANCE

In 1963, America was learning that systems rarely change because one group is right. They change when multiple groups coordinate—when alliance turns conviction into pressure and pressure becomes policy. That's the national inflection: scale is not just volume; it is organization moving in one direction.

Most of us inherit a version of this in private: we try to carry big outcomes with small support, and then mistake exhaustion for failure. Your work is to gather for scale—build alliances that match your assignment, choose partners who share standards, and let your difference become a contribution to a shared outcome rather than a private weight you carry alone.

Difference matters here because it expands what's possible. It forces the coalition to see what it would otherwise miss, and it keeps the mission honest about who "progress" must include. History, once understood, can become prophecy—because alliance is how the wheel moves when one set of hands is not enough.

YOUR WORK (REFLECTION)

Where is your difference trying to tell you the truth?

I'm noticing: ______________________________

I'm naming: ______________________________

I'm choosing: ______________________________

INFLECTION POINT 10: RESURRECTION – 1968

"REBUILD AFTER LOSS."

THE HEADWIND

The time is 1968, and America is trying to hold itself together while something essential is breaking in public. This is not only a year of grief. It is a year of exposure—when the country is forced to look at what prosperity has *not* solved: housing, policing, opportunity, and the unequal geography of safety.

Resurrection, in this context, is not denial. It is the work of rebuilding after loss—of deciding what gets carried forward, what gets repaired, and what can no longer be normalized.

LEADERSHIP CONTEXT

- **President(s):** Lyndon B. Johnson.
- **National posture:** national unrest, major policy movement, and a widening conversation about economic justice—not just civil rights.

BRIEFING

- **What's happening:** the country faces political violence, urban unrest, and urgent demands for economic justice.
- **What shifts structurally:** the nation begins writing new rules in real time—especially around housing and opportunity—while simultaneously revealing the limits of what policy can fix without enforcement and long-term commitment.

POWER & POLICY SIGNALS

- Kerner Commission Report (Feb. 29, 1968) warns the nation about deep structural divides and failed housing and social policy.
- Dr. Martin Luther King Jr. is assassinated (April 4, 1968)—a national rupture that accelerates legislative pressure.
- Civil Rights Act of 1968 / Fair Housing Act signed (April 11, 1968)—housing discrimination is targeted as a national economic issue, not just a local social conflict.
- Poor People's Campaign (May–June 1968) brings a multi-racial economic justice frame into national focus.

MIDDLE-CLASS SNAPSHOT

- The middle class is increasingly defined by stable employment + benefits + homeownership—yet housing is also where inequality hardens into inheritance.
- Neighborhood access (and the credit rules beneath it) becomes one of the clearest dividing lines between "income" and "wealth."

WEALTH VEHICLES

- Home equity remains a dominant engine, making fair access to housing and lending a wealth issue.
- Public-sector and institutional employment ladders continue expanding for many households, functioning as stability platforms.
- Legal enforcement and policy design become "invisible" wealth vehicles—because rules determine who can protect and compound gains.

MILESTONES ACROSS COMMUNITIES (SELECTED)

- **Black communities:** 1968 marks both grief and a policy pivot—housing becomes a national civil-rights battleground, even as enforcement and implementation remain uneven.
- **White communities:** many households continue compounding wealth through protected housing markets and institutional access; policy changes reshape norms, but existing asset advantages remain significant.
- **Latino communities:** the Poor People's Campaign explicitly includes Hispanic Americans, signaling a broader coalition view of economic rights and widening the frame beyond a single community.
- **Asian American communities:** late-1960s reforms and shifting pathways set up later professional-class expansion for some groups, alongside continued intra-group inequality.
- **Indigenous nations/Tribal nations:** the Poor People's Campaign explicitly includes Native Americans, reinforcing that economic justice is not a single-lane

struggle—and that land, resources, and sovereignty remain wealth questions.

- **System note:** 1968 teaches the country that "rights" and "wealth" are not separate conversations when housing and opportunity determine what a household can pass down.

DOCUMENTED BREAKTHROUGHS: WHO MOVED THE WHEEL

- Fair Housing Act (1968)—a direct attempt to interrupt housing discrimination as an inheritance mechanism.
- Shirley Chisholm elected to Congress (1968)—a milestone in institutional access and representation, and a signal that new leadership pathways are opening.

OUR INHERITANCE (KEEP THIS FORMAT)

In 1968, America is learning that loss does not pause the system—it reveals it. That's the national inflection: grief and unrest can either collapse a society into cynicism or force it into reforms that reshape what is possible to inherit.

Most of us inherit a version of this in private: the moment when what we assumed was stable is no longer stable, and we have to rebuild without the comfort of certainty. Your work is to rebuild after loss with discipline—separating what is timeless from what was merely familiar, and choosing structures that can carry your household forward.

Difference matters here because it helps you tell the truth without losing hope. It gives you the clarity to name what failed, the courage to repair what can be repaired, and the imagination to build what has not existed yet. History, once understood, can become prophecy—because rebuilding is where the future gets authored.

YOUR WORK (REFLECTION)

Where is your difference trying to tell you the truth?

I'm noticing: ______________________________

I'm naming: ______________________________

I'm choosing: ______________________________

INFLECTION POINT 11: AUDACITY — 2009–2017 (OBAMA ERA)

"STAND IN INHERITED POSSIBILITY."

THE HEADWIND

The period is 2009–2017, and America is emerging from a financial crisis, its story shaken. The country is trying to recover—markets rising, jobs returning, institutions stabilizing—while households experience the recovery very differently depending on what they owned before the fall.

This is the Obama era: an achievement of national symbolism paired with a test of national structure. A country can elect its first Black president and still reveal, in the numbers, how uneven opportunity remains once the economy starts compounding again.

LEADERSHIP CONTEXT

- **President(s):** Barack Obama (Jan. 20, 2009 - Jan. 20, 2017), the first African American U.S. president.
- **National posture:** post-crisis recovery, institutional reform debates, and a renewed conversation about who the promise reaches in practice.

Briefing

- **What's happening:** the U.S. economy recovers from the Great Recession; asset prices rebound, especially for households positioned to benefit from rising markets.
- **What shifts structurally:** the "recovery" becomes a mirror—revealing portfolio differences (home equity vs. stock exposure), credit access differences, and how quickly wealth can re-separate after a shock.

POWER & POLICY SIGNALS

- Recovery efforts stabilize markets and employment, but wealth rebuilding depends heavily on *which assets you held* and *whether you could hold on through the downturn.*

MIDDLE-CLASS SNAPSHOT

- "Middle class" increasingly means: stable income + benefits + home equity + retirement accounts.
- The gap between income recovery and wealth recovery becomes more visible—especially across race and ethnicity after the recession.

WEALTH VEHICLES

- Home equity (and whether it was wiped out or preserved during the housing crash).
- Stock market exposure (portfolio composition becomes destiny during recovery periods).
- Small business ownership as a wealth lever—but still constrained by capital access and credit terms.
- Retirement plans and institutional ladders that quietly compound over decades.

MILESTONES ACROSS COMMUNITIES (SELECTED)

- **Black communities:** increased college attainment and professional employment for many, alongside a harsh wealth test—Black households were hit hard by housing losses and faced a slower wealth rebound than white households.
- **White communities:** on average, recovered wealth faster after the recession, reflecting higher initial assets and greater exposure to market gains.
- **Latino communities:** growth in entrepreneurship and homeownership in many regions, while also facing elevated vulnerability to housing-cycle shocks and wealth volatility.
- **Asian American communities:** some of the highest median household incomes overall, alongside meaningful intra-group inequality that complicates the "one story" narrative.
- **Indigenous nations / Tribal nations:** continued constraints tied to land, infrastructure investment, and access to capital markets; household and community wealth-building remains deeply shaped by policy and credit conditions.
- **System note:** the era proves a quiet law of compounding: after a crisis, the distance between "having assets" and "having income" matters more than most people realize.

DOCUMENTED BREAKTHROUGHS: WHO MOVED THE WHEEL

- Barack Obama becomes the first Black president—a national symbolic breakthrough that expands perceived possibility and reshapes civic imagination.
- Data clarity on the wealth gap becomes harder to ignore: research shows long-run convergence slowed and later stalled, with the gap widening again after 1980 as capital gains disproportionately benefited white households.
- Post-recession divergence: Pew documents widening racial wealth inequality in the early recovery period.

OUR INHERITANCE

In 2009–2017, America learned that representation can expand imagination, but it does not automatically rewrite structure. That's the national inflection: possibility can be publicly affirmed while wealth outcomes remain privately determined by assets, access, and the ability to stay positioned through volatility.

Most of us inherit a version of this in private: we want the promise to apply to us, but we still have to build the capacity to hold it. Your work is to practice audacity with discipline—claim possibility, yes, but also acquire the vehicles that make possibility durable: ownership, diversified assets, protected credit, and a wealth group that can keep you steady when the cycle turns.

Difference matters here because it keeps you honest about both realities at once: the breakthrough and the burden, the progress and the gap. When you can hold both without denial, you can build without naïveté—and that's where history stops being a headline and starts becoming an inheritance you can redirect. History, once understood, can become prophecy—because audacity, paired with structure, turns "maybe" into "built."

YOUR WORK (REFLECTION)

Where is your difference trying to tell you the truth?

I'm noticing: ______________________________

I'm naming: ______________________________

I'm choosing: ______________________________

DEMOGRAPHIC SHIFT: WHEN "MINORITY" STOPS MEANING WHAT IT USED TO MEAN

"America is becoming a different kind of country. As a result, the meaning of 'being different' is changing. That changes how coalitions form, how markets form, and who gets to own."
--GEORGE PACKER, Staff Writer *The Atlantic*

The 20th century didn't only transform America's economy. It transformed America's composition.

The United States evolved from a predominantly white population to a nation with a rich array of racial and ethnic minorities, and the meaning of "minority" keeps evolving as the century turns. At the start of the century, the United States was overwhelmingly white—about 87%—and the largest nonwhite population was primarily Black Americans concentrated in the rural South. By the century's end, non-Hispanic whites were under 75% of the population, and the country's minority population had changed shape: Hispanics rising to nearly the size of the Black population, Asian communities surging, and a small but growing American Indian population.

And the trajectory continues. The point isn't to recite numbers. The point is to name the shift: by the middle of the 21st century, "minority" is expected to mean something different that is meant in the 20th. (*prb.org*) Looking forward, PRB notes projections where the U.S. becomes more plural in every direction, making "minority" a less useful category and "access" a more important one.

Sanity check (current data anchor): Census' Vintage 2023 estimates put non-Hispanic White at 58% of the U.S. population in 2023, and Hispanics at 19.5%—with Hispanic growth accounting for a large share of overall population growth from 2022–2023. (census.gov)

Why this belongs in a wealth book: because wealth systems don't respond only to ideals. They respond to who is here, who is organized, and who can convert difference into durable ownership.

DIFFERENCE CHANGES THE STARTING LINE. OWNERSHIP CHANGES THE FINISH.

The next decade of wealth will not be defined only by market performance. It will be defined by who is positioned to participate, who is trusted, and who is prepared to hold what is coming.

Multiple research firms are tracking the same macro-shift from different angles: an historic intergenerational transfer, a continued rise in women's control of assets, and a diversification of who is building, inheriting, and governing capital. The point is not symbolic. It is structural.

Cerulli projects $124 trillion in wealth will transfer through 2048. And McKinsey projects U.S. women will control roughly $34 trillion by 2030.

Those two numbers alone tell you what the next decade is really about: asset handoffs at scale—and a widening set of decision-makers who will need trustworthy guidance, clear vehicles, and governance structures that actually match their lives.

This is why inclusion is not simply a social mission. It is a market mandate. When trust expands, opportunity follows.

The Ownership Divide

There is another shift happening underneath the demographic story—one that is easy to miss because it doesn't trend on social media: the dividing line between the asset-owning class and everyone else.

Identity still shapes access in America. It shapes the neighborhoods people can enter, the credit terms they receive, the risks they are expected to carry, and the institutions that welcome—or resist—their participation. But ownership is the multiplier. When assets compound, the gap compounds.

Federal Reserve distributional data tracks how wealth concentrates over time, including the share held by the bottom half of households. The numbers don't argue; they reveal. If you want a different kind of wealth, the assignment is not only to earn more. It is to own more wisely—and to build protections so what you gain can be kept and grown.

And that is exactly why the next inflection point is Ownership.

SOURCES

- Cerulli: projected $124T wealth transfer through 2048.
- McKinsey: projected ~$34T U.S. women-controlled assets by 2030.
- Federal Reserve (via FRED DFA series): wealth/asset distribution tracking (bottom 50% share).

INFLECTION POINT 12: OWNERSHIP — 2019–PRESENT

"TAKE POSSESSION."

THE HEADWIND

The time is 2019–present, and America is living inside overlapping shocks—pandemic disruption, an inflation cycle, rapid rate changes, platform-driven markets, and a cultural renegotiation of who gets seen as "investable." The economy didn't just speed up. The *rules* got louder. More households now recognize what used to be whispered: income is survival, but ownership is freedom—because ownership is what compounds when you're not looking.

This is an ownership era because the question isn't simply, *Can you earn?* It's: Can you hold? Can you govern? Can you compound without gambling?

LEADERSHIP CONTEXT

- **President(s):** Trump → Biden.
- **National posture:** volatility + reinvention; households and institutions testing what holds under pressure.

BRIEFING

- **What's happening:** people experience multiple cycles at once—asset booms and reversals, housing affordability whiplash, higher borrowing costs, workplace shifts, and rising entrepreneurial experimentation.
- **What shifts structurally:** ownership becomes a literacy test. Those who understand vehicles, risk, and protections gain options. Those who don't become more exposed, even if their income rises.

POWER & POLICY SIGNALS

- Emergency economic intervention during the pandemic teaches a modern lesson: policy can stabilize households fast—but it can't replace long-term asset strategy.
- Investor protections and fiduciary expectations are sharpening (people increasingly ask, "Are you advising me, or selling to me?").
- Rate and inflation regimes reset the math of borrowing, saving, and homeownership—making timing and structure more decisive than hustle alone.

MIDDLE-CLASS SNAPSHOT

- The middle class is still "the package": steady income, benefits, some home equity, retirement assets, and the hope of upward mobility.
- But the package costs more now—housing, childcare, healthcare, and debt service—and many households feel the difference between *working hard* and *owning well.*

WEALTH VEHICLES

- Home equity (still central, but highly sensitive to rates and timing).
- Retirement systems (401(k)/IRA) as default compounding engines.
- Index funds + ETFs as mainstream market access.
- Alternatives (private credit, private real estate, private equity access via new platforms)—more available, more complex, more fee-sensitive.
- Digital assets for some households—high volatility, high narrative power, uneven outcomes.
- Business ownership as a wealth vehicle *and* a governance test (cash flow, taxes, risk, protections).

MILESTONES ACROSS COMMUNITIES (SELECTED)

(All segments included—because Ownership is where every "starting line" meets the same compounding rules.)

- **Black communities:** intensified focus on closing the racial wealth gap; growth in Black entrepreneurship; expanding attention to capital access, home appraisal fairness, and ownership pathways that don't require permission.
- **White communities:** continued concentration of household wealth overall; rising awareness that stability can be fragile when it's built mostly on one vehicle (housing) or one assumption (low rates).
- **Latino communities:** major drivers of household formation and small-business creation; homeownership framed as a central intergenerational lever—often constrained by affordability, credit terms, and regional market conditions.

- **Asian American communities:** strong income performance for many, alongside meaningful intra-group inequality; accelerated intergenerational transfer conversations; rising demand for culturally fluent advice and planning.
- **Indigenous nations / Tribal nations:** renewed focus on sovereignty-linked economic development, land governance, and community-based wealth tools; ownership questions often intersect policy, resource control, and long-horizon stewardship.
- **Women-led households (cross-cutting):** rising control of assets and decision-making authority; increased visibility of the "default advisor gap" (who gets trusted, who gets served, and who is still under-advised).
- **System note:** ownership is increasingly shaped by literacy + legal structure + networks + timing—not effort alone.

DOCUMENTED BREAKTHROUGHS: WHO MOVED THE WHEEL

- **A cultural shift:** wealth stops being a private subject and becomes a public one, especially for those who have been excluded from compounding vehicles and why.
- **A market shift:** broader participation tools (low-cost funds, fractional access, digital platforms) expand ownership possibilities, while also expanding complexity and noise.
- **A trust shift:** the next era of advisory growth belongs to those who can translate the system without condescension—so more households can participate without being preyed upon.

OUR INHERITANCE

In 2019–present, America is learning that ownership is not a finish line—it is a set of choices repeated under pressure. That's the national inflection: volatility doesn't just test portfolios; it tests systems, relationships, and the stories people believe about what they deserve and what they can hold.

Most of us inherit a version of this in private. Many of us learned to chase outcomes, but were not always taught the structures that make outcomes sustainable. We learned to work for stability, without always learning how to govern what we build. Ownership requires a different kind of attention—the kind that turns progress into something that lasts. Your work is to take possession of your numbers, your vehicles, your risks, your protections, and your people—so wealth becomes governed, not guessed.

Your difference matters here because it sharpens design. It helps you build in a way that fits your real life, your real community, and your real constraints—without borrowing someone else's blueprint and calling it discipline. When you can see the wheel clearly, you stop arguing with gravity and start building with it. And that is where history, once understood, becomes something you can finally direct.

YOUR WORK (REFLECTION)

Where is your difference trying to tell you the truth?

I'm noticing: ______________________________

I'm naming: ______________________________

I'm choosing: ______________________________

Bonus prompt: What is the next "possession" move you can make on paper this week—one number, one account, one protection, or one decision you can finally name?

SOURCES BY INFLECTION POINT

1) VALUE (1619 — JAMESTOWN)

- [1] Reuters — Timeline of Racial Wealth Gap.
- [2] Princeton GCEPS — Wealth of Two Nations: The U.S. Racial Wealth Gap, 1860–2020.

2) FREEDOM (1776)

- [2] Princeton GCEPS — Wealth of Two Nations.
- [3] AFL-CIO — historical overview (wealth gap context).
- [4] Britannica Kids — African American history timeline (free Black community anchors).

3) PERSPECTIVE (1861–1865 — CIVIL WAR)

- [2] Princeton GCEPS — Wealth of Two Nations: The U.S. Racial Wealth Gap, 1860–2020.
- [3] AFL-CIO — history overview (wealth gap context).
- [5] Wikipedia — civil rights movement (1865–1896) (used as a timeline reference).

4) PIVOT (1865–1895 — RECONSTRUCTION)

- [1] Reuters — Timeline of Racial Wealth Gap.
- [2] Princeton GCEPS — Wealth of Two Nations.

- [3] AFL-CIO — historical overview.
- [6] Jim Crow Museum (Ferris State) — Reconstruction timeline.

5) PURSUIT (1896)

- [2] Princeton GCEPS — Wealth of Two Nations: The U.S. Racial Wealth Gap, 1860–2020.
- [3] AFL-CIO — historical overview (wealth gap context).
- [4] Britannica Kids — African American history timeline (accessible anchors for era framing).
- [6] Jim Crow Museum (Ferris State) — Reconstruction/Jim Crow timeline framing (segregation-era context).
- [1] Reuters — Timeline of Racial Wealth Gap (optional but strong as a macro timeline anchor; include if you want one "big picture" source per inflection point).

6) PARTNER (1909)

- NAACP founding (1909; Feb 12; founding context and early mission).
- U.S. Census Bureau, History and the Census: The 1909 Founding of the NAACP.
- NAACP, Our History.
- History.com, The NAACP is founded.
- Charles Hamilton Houston (strategic legal architecture; Howard Law; paving the way toward desegregation litigation).
- NAACP, Charles Hamilton Houston.
- Asian American exclusion context shaping "institutional access" (background for the era's "niches under constraint" language).
- Encyclopaedia Britannica, Chinese Exclusion Act.

7) MIGRATION (1939)

- [2] Princeton GCEPS — Wealth of Two Nations: The U.S. Racial Wealth Gap, 1860–2020.
- [3] AFL-CIO — historical overview (wealth gap and policy context).
- [4] Britannica Kids — African American history timeline (Great Migration anchors).
- [8] PMC article — Latino migrant economic outcomes (used for broader framing).
- [9] Civitas Institute — *The Rise of Latino America* (demographic/economic framing).
- [7] NBER — Asian American mobility/discrimination framing.
- [10] EPI — AAPI economic disparities (intra-group inequality + pathways).

8) PATIENT POWER (1954)

- [2] Princeton GCEPS — Wealth of Two Nations: The U.S. Racial Wealth Gap, 1860–2020.
- [3] AFL-CIO — historical overview (wealth gap and policy context).
- [4] Britannica Kids — African American history timeline (Brown/civil rights anchors).
- [5] Wikipedia — civil rights movement (1865–1896) (used cautiously; better replaced with a primary/encyclopedia source for Brown in final pass).
- [7] NBER — Asian American mobility/discrimination framing.
- [8] PMC article — Latino migrant economic outcomes (broad framing).

- [9] Civitas Institute – The Rise of Latino America.
- [10] EPI – AAPI economic disparities (for intra-group dynamics and pathways).

9) ALLIANCE (1963)

- National Archives – March on Washington overview; official program document.
- Smithsonian – 1963 March on Washington context and goals.
- Britannica – March on Washington summary and significance.
- History.com – March on Washington overview.
- Wikipedia (reference only) – *The Fire Next Time* publication year (1963).
- Wikipedia (reference only) – INA 1965 signed Oct. 3, 1965 (for later-era pathway note).

10) RESURRECTION (1968)

- Kerner Commission Report released (Feb. 29, 1968) – History.com.
- MLK assassination (April 4, 1968) – History.com.
- Fair Housing Act / Title VIII signed April 11, 1968 – Britannica; DOJ Civil Rights Division.
- Civil Rights Act of 1968 signed April 11, 1968 – AP (Today in History).
- Poor People's Campaign (1968) – Britannica.
- Shirley Chisholm elected to Congress (1968) – Britannica video explainer; Wikipedia (reference).

11) AUDACITY (2009–2017)

- Britannica – Obama was the 44th president (2009–17) and the first African American to hold the office.
- Pew Research Center (2014)—racial wealth gaps widened in the Great Recession's aftermath; white median wealth far exceeds Black and Hispanic median wealth (SCF-based).
- Russell Sage Foundation report page—Wealth of Two Nations: The U.S. Racial Wealth Gap, 1860–2020 (abstract + key claims).
- NBER working paper page—*Wealth of Two Nations* (paper metadata + framing; persistent gap; role of capital gains).
- Princeton Economics working paper summary page—highlights periods of convergence and stall since the 1980s.

12) OWNERSHIP (2019–PRESENT)

Named Receipt: Regulation Best Interest (Reg BI) – compliance date June 30, 2020

- SEC Small Business Compliance Guide (states effective date and compliance date June 30, 2020).
- SEC Chairman Jay Clayton's statement confirming June 30, 2020, compliance date for Reg BI and Form CRS (June 15, 2020).
- SEC statement noting the "four-month anniversary" of the June 30 Reg BI and Form CRS compliance date (Oct. 26, 2020).

Ownership divide data anchor (distribution/compounding context)

- FRED (Federal Reserve Distributional Financial Accounts): *Share of Financial Assets Held by the Bottom 50%* (series WFRBSB50193; notes explain DFA methodology).

Policy shock marker (pandemic-era intervention; optional but clean if referenced)

- U.S. Treasury: CARES Act passed March 25, 2020; signed March 27, 2020 (official overview page).
- Treasury OIG CARES Act page also states signed into law March 27, 2020 (secondary Treasury-domain corroboration).

America learned that outcomes follow structure. Most of us inherited patterns we didn't choose—how we think about money, who we trust, what we fear, and what we normalize. Your work is to build with intention: a wealth group, a set of protections, and a portfolio of vehicles that fit your life. Let your difference become discernment—of people, policies, and tradeoffs—until it becomes ownership of your resources and your legacy. That's how history, once understood, can become prophecy.

BIBLIOGRAPHY

ECONOMICS, CAPITAL, AND SYSTEMS

- Smith, Adam. The Wealth of Nations (1776).
- Fukuyama, Francis. Trust: The Social Virtues and the Creation of Prosperity.
- Howe, Neil & Strauss, William. *The Fourth Turning*.
- Diamond, Jared. *Guns, Germs, and Steel* (for meta-pattern context).

HISTORY, RACE, AND AMERICAN STRUCTURE

- Baldwin, James. *The Fire Next Time*: *I Am Not Your Negro*.
- Du Bois, W.E.B. Black Reconstruction in America.
- Wilkerson, Isabel. The Warmth of Other Suns.
- Alexander, Michelle. *The New Jim Crow*.
- Rothstein, Richard. *The Color of Law*.

TRAUMA, MEMORY, AND THE BODY

- Rothschild, Babette. *The Body Remembers*.
- van der Kolk, Bessel. *The Body Keeps the Score*.

FAITH, ETHICS, AND MORAL IMAGINATION

- The Holy Bible (*Genesis, Exodus, Joshua, Jeremiah, Luke).*
- *King Jr., Martin Luther. Where Do We Go From Here?*
- *Niebuhr, Reinhold. Moral* Man and Immoral Society.

CIVIC KNOWLEDGE AND DEMOCRACY

- Annenberg Pub*lic Policy Center. Civics Knowledge Surveys.*
- *U.S. Constitution* & Amendments.

ABOUT THE AUTHOR

Dr. Pamela Jolly is a thought leader, cultural critic, and architect of frameworks that sit at the intersection of history, wealth, belief, and collective impact.

An uncommon range of experiences shapes her work: four academic degrees spanning business, theology, and research; decades of disciplined study across thousands of books; and a career that has carried her across the United States and internationally in pursuit of a single question—*what actually allows people to build wealth that lasts?*

Along the way, she learned that wealth is not simply an economic outcome.
It is a choice.
A choice shaped by belief.
A choice revealed through action.
And a choice that compounds when pursued collectively.

Dr. Jolly has worked inside financial institutions, corporate environments, faith communities, nonprofit systems, entrepreneurial ventures, and academic spaces. She has advised leaders, taught cohorts, built businesses, chaired boards, and conducted research that required listening deeply to how people understand success, freedom, risk, and responsibility. What emerged was not another theory of money, but a pattern—a recurring truth visible across generations, industries, and cultures.

That truth is this:
People do not fail to build wealth because they lack ability.
They fail because they do not fully own their difference.

Through years of observation, teaching, and lived experience, Dr. Jolly came to see that belief drives action—and that action, when aligned with an accepted and understood sense of one's unique value, creates momentum powerful enough to move families, communities, and institutions forward. When that momentum is shared—within tribes, churches, industries, neighborhoods, or movements—it becomes legacy.

Her work challenges the idea that wealth is individualistic, accidental, or reserved for a few. Instead, she advances a vision of wealth as a group process, one that requires clarity of position, shared standards, and the courage to act without waiting for permission.

Dr. Jolly is the creator of the NarrowRoad™ framework, which helps individuals and groups identify their distinct perspectives, convert belief into disciplined action, and pursue outcomes they believe in—together. Her voice is shaped as much by history as by lived reality, as attentive to cultural patterns as to personal responsibility.

A Different Kind of Wealth reflects her deepest conviction:

That every generation inherits both a burden and an opportunity.

That the way forward is often found by looking back with honesty.

And that is when people accept the value of their difference—and fund it with action—they can take possession of their promised land, not alone, but together.

REGISTER YOUR COPY OF A DIFFERENT KIND OF WEALTH

by Pamela C. V. Jolly

Unlock reader bonuses, stay encouraged as you read, and help others begin their own wealth journey.

You've taken an important step by picking up this book.

Register your copy to receive:

- Short, practical reflection prompts that help you apply each chapter.
- Encouragement and insights to help you stay engaged as life gets busy.
- Invitations to conversations, experiences, and future resources connected to the book.
- A simple way to invite friends, family, churches, organizations, or communities to read together.

BECAUSE WEALTH WAS NEVER MEANT TO BE BUILT ALONE.

Or visit:

https://www.pamelajolly.com/adkw-register-your-copy

The journey continues with what you choose to build next.

The NarrowRoad™ is a framework for understanding wealth as more than money.

Developed through decades of work in finance, community development, leadership, and theological study, the NarrowRoad™ explores how individuals, families, organizations, and communities create lasting outcomes through the intentional development of multiple forms of capital.

At the heart of the framework is a simple idea:

Wealth is the ability to create the future you believe in.

Money matters, but it is only one resource among many.

The NarrowRoad™ recognizes five forms of capital that shape our lives and influence our ability to build a meaningful legacy:

HUMAN CAPITAL

The knowledge, skills, talents, health, and capabilities we develop throughout our lives.

SOCIAL CAPITAL

The relationships, networks, trust, and connections that make collective progress possible.

CULTURAL CAPITAL

The traditions, values, stories, and lived experiences that shape identity and belonging.

INTELLECTUAL CAPITAL

The ideas, innovations, wisdom, and insights that generate new possibilities.

SPIRITUAL CAPITAL

The beliefs, purpose, convictions, and sense of calling that guide decisions and sustain perseverance.

Throughout *A Different Kind of Wealth*, the twelve inflection points serve as lenses through which readers can examine how these forms of capital have been developed, challenged, exchanged, protected, and expanded across generations.

The goal is not simply to understand history.

The goal is to discover how your own difference can become a contribution—one that helps build a future worthy of those who came before and those who will follow.

www.ingramcontent.com/pod-product-compliance
Lightning Source LLC
LaVergne TN
LVHW020413220926
848484LV00017B/2558/J
* 9 7 8 1 9 6 7 6 7 4 5 3 4 *